12/11

D1450815

CONTROVERSY!

Identity
Theft

Rachael Hanel

Marion Carnegie Library
206 S. Market St
Marion. IL 62959

Marshall Cavendish
Benchmark
New York

Copyright © 2011 Marshall Cavendish Corporation
Published by Marshall Cavendish Benchmark
An imprint of Marshall Cavendish Corporation

All rights reserved.
No part of this publication may be reproduced, stored in a retrieval system or transmitted,
in any form or by any means, electronic, mechanical, photocopying, recording, or otherwise,
without the prior permission of the copyright owner. Request for permission should be addressed to
the Publisher, Marshall Cavendish Corporation, 99 White Plains Road, Tarrytown, NY 10591.
Tel: (914) 332-8888, fax: (914) 332-1888.
Website: www.marshallcavendish.us

This publication represents the opinions and views of the author based on
Rachael Hanel's personal experience, knowledge, and research. The information in this book
serves as a general guide only. The author and publisher have used their best efforts in
preparing this book and disclaim liability rising directly and
indirectly from the use and application of this book.

Other Marshall Cavendish Offices:
Marshall Cavendish International (Asia) Private Limited, 1 New Industrial Road,
Singapore 536196 • Marshall Cavendish International (Thailand) Co Ltd. 253 Asoke, 12th Flr,
Sukhumvit 21 Road, Klongtoey Nua, Wattana, Bangkok 10110, Thailand •
Marshall Cavendish (Malaysia) Sdn Bhd, Times Subang, Lot 46, Subang Hi-Tech Industrial Park,
Batu Tiga, 40000 Shah Alam, Selangor Darul Ehsan, Malaysia

Marshall Cavendish is a trademark of Times Publishing Limited
All websites were available and accurate when this book was sent to press.

Library of Congress Cataloging-in-Publication Data
Hanel, Rachael. • Identity theft / Rachael Hanel.—1st ed.
p. cm.— (Controversy!) • Includes bibliographical references and index.
ISBN 978-0-7614-4901-0
1. Identity theft—Juvenile literature. I. Title.
HV6675.H29 2011 • 364.16'33 — dc22 • 2009033403

Publisher: Michelle Bisson • Art Director: Anahid Hamparian
Series Designer: Alicia Mikles • Photo research by Lindsay Aveilhe

The photographs in this book are used by permission and through the courtesy of:
Paul Barton/Corbis: cover; Fotosearch: 4; Karin Lau/Alamy: 8; Newscom: 16; Dennis Cook/AP
Photo: 20; Andrea Mohin/The New York Times/Redux: 26; William Perlman/Star Ledger/Corbis:
34; Melanie Stetson Freeman/The Christian Science Monitor via Getty Images: 37; Bob Johns/
expresspictures.co.uk/Alamy: 40; Gentry Mullen/Newscom: 50; Stephanie Carter/Glow Images:
58; Michael Stravato/The New York Times/Redux: 61; Scott Myers/Rex Features/Courtesy Everett
Collection: 65; Rafael Diaz/EFE/Corbis: 68; Reed Saxon/AP Photo: 71; Tim Boyle/Getty Images:
74; Paul J. Richards/AFP/Getty Images: 95; AP Photo/Chuck Stoody: 97; Andrew Brookes/Cor-
bis: 99; Chris Young/Pool/Reuters/Corbis: 106; China Foto Daily: 109; Sipa Press/Newscom: 113

Printed in Malaysia (T)
135642

Contents

IDENTITY THEFT

Identity theft is one of the fastest-growing crimes in the United States. Fear of being a victim of such a crime has led to an upsurge in the shredding of personal information to save it from the hands of thieves.

Introduction

A POLICE OFFICER STOPS A YOUNG MAN FOR speeding. After running the driver's license through a database, the officer discovers that there is a warrant issued for the driver's arrest for stolen vehicles and drug possession. But the driver has never committed a criminal act in his life. He realizes that someone must have obtained his driver's license information and committed crimes in his name. He spends a night in jail before he is able to gather enough personal documentation to prove to police that someone else has been using his identity. He has been treated like a criminal, even though he has not committed a crime.

A man gets a call from his credit card company. The customer service representative had noticed a series of strange charges occurring over a period of several days from many different states. She wants to know if the cardholder made those purchases. He says no, and thanks the woman for alerting him to the fraud. He's grateful that the credit card company could track his personal information to uncover the fraudulent transactions, but it makes him wonder who else might be tracking his data.

A woman receives a stern notice from the Internal Revenue Service (IRS). The government agency is asking her to pay thousands of dollars in back taxes on income received for a series of jobs. But the woman does not recognize the employers' names, nor has she ever lived in the states where the employers are based.

She calls the IRS for more information and discovers that someone has been using her Social Security number to obtain employment. Like nearly all U.S. residents, she has revealed her Social Security number over and over on job applications, credit card applications, and on medical forms. From which of these was her Social Security number taken? Will she ever find out?

Thousands of customers of a company receive a letter in the mail. The letter states that the company's database has been corrupted, and people's credit card numbers may have fallen into the wrong hands. Customers are encouraged to cut up their old cards and obtain new cards with new account numbers. Should they go through the inconvenience of closing old accounts and starting new ones? How high is the risk to their information?

These are just a few of many ways that identity theft is perpetrated around the globe. Identity thieves may target one individual, or they may form a massive crime ring and obtain personal information from thousands of people. Identity thieves might lift one credit card from a wallet to commit their crimes, or they might invest thousands of dollars in sophisticated equipment to steal information in high-tech ways.

Identity theft is one of the fastest-growing crimes in the United States. The U.S. Department of Justice notes that identity theft is quickly gaining on drug trafficking as the number one crime in the nation. One report puts the cost of identity theft in the United States for one year at $49.3 billion.

However identity theft occurs, and for whatever reason, one thing is certain: millions of people every year find themselves victimized. The Federal Trade Commission (FTC) estimates that nearly 9 million adults have their identities stolen each year.

Few people realize how much information is compiled about them and how it is used. Banks, credit card companies, employers, and government agencies are just a few of the organizations that keep personal data on file. With the vast amount of information out there, it is no wonder that this data sometimes falls into the wrong hands. How to protect this data, and in which cases to make it available, can raise controversy regarding privacy and civil liberties.

The good news is that individuals and businesses can take steps to prevent identity theft. The more people know about identity theft and how to protect themselves, the fewer opportunities criminals have to commit their crimes.

Identity theft occurs in all sorts of ways. One of the easiest, despite its carrying a federal penalty if caught, is to break into a mailbox and steal personal information.

1 What Is Identity Theft?

SIMPLY PUT, IDENTITY THEFT IS THE UNLAWFUL USE of someone else's personal information. This personal information can be used in many ways, including securing credit, making purchases, obtaining medical services, getting jobs, or evading criminal investigation. This is not an exhaustive list: there are many reasons that someone would steal another person's identity.

Identity theft is a growing problem that costs people billions of dollars each year. Victims pay the price in numerous ways: ruined credit, resulting in the inability to obtain loans for cars and homes; hours spent trying to rectify the situation; even criminal investigations in which they are the target.

Statistics highlight the scope of the problem. The most recent comprehensive survey commissioned by the Federal Trade Commission was completed in 2006. That survey found that 3.7 percent of the adult population in the United States reported being victims of identity theft. While this small percentage represents roughly 8.3 million people, the concern is the large amounts of money lost because of such crimes, the ruined credit of so many consumers, and the potential damage an identity thief can do to others if not caught.

In terms of money lost, the median value of goods obtained in someone else's name was $500. (A median value means that half of the people reported more than $500 in fraudulent purchases, while the other half reported less than $500). But 10 percent of victims reported that the criminals obtained more than $6,000 in goods.

Victims report that the thefts have left them questioning the security of their data. Many had taken for granted the idea that their information would be protected. In addition, it takes time and money to recover from identity theft. Targeted consumers often spend hours and hundreds of dollars to resolve the damage to their name and credit. Ten percent of victims say they spent more than 55 hours and $1,200 resolving the issue. And damage often involves more than money and time. About one-third of identity theft victims say that they continued to have problems getting credit and/or loans, have had utilities shut off, and have been targets of criminal investigations. Some have even been arrested for crimes committed by others in their names.

History of Identity Theft

Technology makes our lives easier in many ways. We can quickly make purchases, obtain credit, and check bank statements over the Internet. Unfortunately, this technology also makes it easier for thieves to steal information. This is why identity theft is a growing problem. Identity theft is not new. Scheming thieves have always found ways to take someone's identity and live as someone else as a way to avoid their own crimes or obtain possessions in someone else's name. In 1923 a New Orleans man named Harry Wolfe was canoeing with a friend, Jacob Arnof, when Arnof drowned. Wolfe did not report the death to police. Instead, he assumed Arnof's identity, even going so far as to mark his own face to mimic a scar that Arnof bore. Wolfe, as Arnof, sent messages to Arnof's father and obtained money from family bank accounts. Before committing suicide after he was caught perpetrating another crime, Wolfe confessed his identity theft scheme.

When the telephone became more common in the twentieth century, thieves used the new technology to obtain personal information. One common scam involved calling people to tell them that they had won a prize. The caller asked the victim for personal information, such as a Social Security number or birthday, to verify his or her identity in order to claim the prize. The caller then had enough information to create a financial account using the newly obtained name.

Another common identity theft technique that was around long before the Internet is to rifle through someone's mail or trash. A mailbox can contain a wealth of personal information, from billing statements to credit card offers. If unwanted mail is thrown away intact, someone going through garbage may find account statements and addresses. The technique is called "dumpster diving." This low-tech way of gathering personal information is so reliable that thieves still use it today. The thought of going through garbage may be disgusting, but identity thieves will stop at nothing, especially if the reward ends up being possessions and goods that they do not have to pay for.

Another tried-and-true method for stealing information is to grab someone's wallet or purse. A wallet or purse often contains credit cards, a driver's license, a Social Security number, and blank checks—enough information to get a thief well on his way to assuming a new identity.

Who's at Risk?

Identity theft can strike anyone at any time. No one—old or young, male or female, white, black, or Latino—is immune to this crime. However, reports suggest that certain populations and age groups are more susceptible than others.

In 2008 the highest percentage of identity theft victims—nearly 25 percent—fell between the ages of twenty and twenty-nine. But those nineteen and under and seventy and over made up about half that number of victims in that same year. In many ways, minors and the elderly are the most vulnerable to identity theft; they are unlikely to check their records or lack the capabilities or awareness to do so.

Children

The Federal Trade Commission reports that identity theft cases involving children are increasing. Between 2003 and 2004, reports of this type increased 58 percent. In some cases, parents use their children's Social Security numbers to obtain credit cards or set up utility service. Credit card applications are easy to fill out. Applicants fill in a name, address, and Social Security number, and often no one verifies the age or identity of the applicant. One criticism of these is they open the door to identity theft.

Thieves target children for two reasons: they have a fresh credit history, and it can take years before anyone discovers the crime. For example, the theft of a child's identity may not be known for several years, until that child applies for credit cards and school or car loans. Zach Friesen was seventeen years old when a prospective employer ran a credit report on him and discovered he was $40,000 in debt. Someone had stolen Friesen's identity when he was seven years old, used his name to buy a large boat, and never paid the loan. Friesen now travels the country educating teens and other young adults about the dangers of identity theft.

Parents and guardians should be aware of warning signs that someone may be using a child's identity. For example, the child may start receiving credit card applications, bills, or bank statements in the mail. Debt collectors might call and ask to speak to the child. And when the time comes for an older child to finally open an account, there may be an account already open at a bank in his or her name.

The Elderly

The elderly can be vulnerable to identity theft from caregivers or adult children. For elderly people who are losing mental capabilities, including the capability to handle and understand their own finances, the court will appoint a legal guardian. The guardian is usually a family member or close friend. But this legal guardianship can open the doors to financial abuse. Guardians have access to all of the person's personal and financial data. Guardians can easily use the person's Social Security number or fill out credit card applications that come in the mail without anyone else knowing about it.

The National Center on Elder Abuse has found that financial abuse makes up 21 percent of all elder abuse investigations. Identity theft of elders by relatives or trusted friends may be one of the most underreported forms of identity theft. Victims are often reluctant to pursue criminal charges against family members. They may think that somehow it is their fault. Seeing a child go to jail can add stress to an already stressful and confusing time.

The Dead

Another target for identity thieves is a more unusual one: the recently deceased. Criminals scour obituary notices online and in newspapers and may attempt to take over the identity of someone who has just died. They call widows or widowers claiming to be medical facility representatives and ask for Social Security numbers and birth dates to "finalize paperwork." Criminals use a dead person's Social Security number for all the same reasons they use a living person's data: to buy goods, secure credit, and get jobs. In the case of obtaining employment, people may never discover that a false Social Security number has been used as long as taxes are paid on wages earned.

Stealing a dead person's identity is called "ghosting." Thieves do this because it is hard to detect: the actual victim cannot alert authorities. Stealing the identity of the deceased does not harm that person, but it can harm relatives left behind. Creditors may eventually come after the relatives, seeking payment on unpaid charges. Relatives are the ones who are responsible for resolving the situation. It can cause them financial and psychological harm at an already vulnerable time.

College Students

According to the Federal Trade Commission, nearly one in three identity theft victims is between the ages of eighteen and twenty-nine. And a high number of those victims are college students. College students can be easy targets for a number of reasons. For one, they may not know much about identity theft and how to protect themselves. They are also of a generation that has always been technologically comfortable. They take tests online and fill out job applications and college applications online. They are used to sharing personal information with friends, acquaintances, and even strangers through social networking sites such as Facebook.

Students' names and personal information can be found in all types of college and university databases and in federal loan databases. One out of five identity theft scams happens at a university or college, according to the Identity Theft Resource Center, a clearinghouse of information for victims, law enforcement officials, and the media. In one case, University of California-Los Angeles (UCLA) officials discovered a breach in a database in December 2006. Hackers gained access to information for more than 800,000 students, faculty, staff, and alumni. The hacking took place over a number of months before being discovered. A UCLA official said that fewer than 5 percent of database names were at a higher risk than others for identity theft, but that still involved more than 40,000 people. In March 2009 Iona College in New Rochelle, New York, was the first to install a "breach-free" database with software to detect breaches and help protect students, faculty, and staff against identity theft. Notices would go out immediately if there were a breach. The program also provides financial literacy education and teaches students how to guard their personal information.

College students are frequent targets of credit card companies.

When they walk through a student union, they often are bombarded with requests from credit card company representatives to fill out applications. Credit card companies see college students as a prime source of business. Having credit for the first time tempts a person to spend more money than he or she may have. Students may run up large bills and find they can only afford to make minimum payments. The credit card companies often charge high interest rates on account balances, which is how the companies profit. Sitting next to those legitimate companies at student union card tables may be scammers waiting to pounce and obtain a student's personal information. In addition, college students frequently receive credit card offers in the mail. If they throw away the offers without shredding them, someone going through the trash can steal and fill out the applications.

College students often move from place to place, so any type of information that is mailed to them has the potential to fall into the wrong hands. Students are advised to manage accounts online so sensitive numbers do not go out in the mail.

Another reason students may fall victim more often is that they might not know much about money management and fail to check their account statements regularly. If something is amiss, it may be several months before the student realizes what has been going on.

Many students prefer laptop to desktop computers because they are convenient and portable, but they are also easier to steal because they are so light and portable. A laptop can contain a gold mine of personal information. If laptops are password-protected and engraved with ownership information, identity theft is less likely to occur.

Businesses

Not only are individuals at risk, but so are businesses. Individuals are a source of just one set of personal data. On the other hand, a business can store hundreds, thousands, or even hundreds of

When caught, some hackers help corporations figure out how to stop thieves. This former hacker, part of a network once responsible for cracking everything from Fortune 500 companies to government institutions, demonstrates techniques used in identity theft.

thousands of names and account numbers in one central database. Thieves greedily hope to capitalize on this wealth of data. As a result, many identities are stolen in a workplace setting. Identity theft experts contend that 50 to 70 percent of all identities stolen may have been obtained from a workplace.

Workplace identity theft can occur in many ways: an unethical human resources worker perusing records, a janitor rifling through papers dumped in the trash, or a hacker gaining access to employee records. Statistics show that 75 percent of workplace identity theft is done by someone within the company.

The Identity Theft Resource Center has estimated that one stolen business laptop computer can cost a company $90,000 in fines, legal fees, and credit monitoring services for people whose data may have been compromised.

Businesses themselves can be targets of identity thieves. Businesses are assigned a variety of identification numbers, just as individuals are. These numbers include federal employer identification numbers, Department of the Treasury numbers, and tax identification numbers. Business numbers are used the same way individual numbers are: to access existing accounts or to open new ones.

How It Occurs

Just as physical characteristics—such as hair color, eye color, and height—make each person unique, every person has a set of data that is unique to him or her. If this information falls into the wrong hands, it can allow a thief to assume someone else's identity for criminal purposes. Here is a closer look at what type of information is vulnerable to thieves.

Social Security Number

Upon birth, citizenship, or permanent residency, the U.S. Social Security Administration assigns everyone a nine-digit Social Security number. The government uses this number for tax purposes. Children receive Social Security numbers so parents can claim them as dependents on tax forms. Over the past few years, Social Security numbers have been used as a primary identification for a variety of purposes. The numbers can be found on employment documents, Social Security Administration statements, credit applications, in some student databases, medical records, and on some direct deposit pay stubs. A thief who knows where to look can easily obtain someone's Social Security number. Obtaining a Social Security number is like getting a password. Once a thief has a Social Security number, he or she can do almost anything with it—apply for credit, get a job, open a bank account, and file tax information. Often agencies do not match Social Security numbers with birth dates to verify identities.

Just because someone asks for a Social Security number does not mean a person has to provide it. There are only two reasons to give out Social Security numbers: to an employer (who needs the number for tax purposes), and to financial institutions, such as credit card companies and banks. If others ask for it, a person should always ask why the information is needed and how the number will be used. If a clerk is insistent, a person can fill in the Social Security field on an application with all zeros, or make up a number starting with "78" or "79"—those are not valid starting numbers for real Social Security numbers.

Never carry a Social Security card in a wallet or purse. It should be kept in a safe (preferably locked) location at home.

Personal Identification Numbers

Personal identification numbers (PINs) are most often used at automated teller machines (ATMs). A person swipes a debit or credit card and then is asked to punch in a PIN on a keypad. Thieves obtain PINs in many ways. In some cases, they are easily stolen along with a card because people have written them down instead of memorizing them. At other times, thieves sit at a place where they can watch an ATM, or they may set up a camera near an ATM to capture information. If a thief with a stolen card also knows the PIN, he or she can withdraw money from a victim's account.

Driver's License Number

A driver's license is used as a primary identification. Besides being required to drive a car, it is used to verify a person's identity when cashing checks, voting, and boarding commercial airline flights. All a thief needs to make a phony driver's license is a driver's license number. Sophisticated technology allows thieves to create documents such as driver's licenses that appear authentic. A criminal can take a driver's license number and make a new license with his or her own picture on it. That's all it takes to start living a life as someone else.

Passwords

In today's technologically rich society, a person may have dozens of passwords for different accounts and websites. People pay bills, do their banking, and order merchandise online. Each online account requires a password. Once a thief has a user name and a password, he or she can unlock all types of information associated with an account. He can start buying merchandise in someone else's name or hijack valuable financial data. Identity thieves can sometimes guess passwords, especially if people have used birth dates, children's names, or pets' names to create passwords. Passwords are tougher to crack when they include a combination of letters, numbers, and special characters (such as #, $, or %).

Other Sensitive Information

Thieves also can make use of a birth date or a mother's maiden name. This information by itself will not get a criminal very far, but in combination with a password, PIN, or Social Security number, many more opportunities for crime will open up. Credit card or loan applications often ask for a Social Security number and a birth date, or a Social Security number and a mother's maiden name (in theory, for security and identification purposes).

Some Surprising Places

Identity theft can show up when people least expect it. Any place that lists a name and other personal information, such as a birth date, a telephone number, or email address, opens the door to potential identity thieves. Thieves do not need credit card numbers

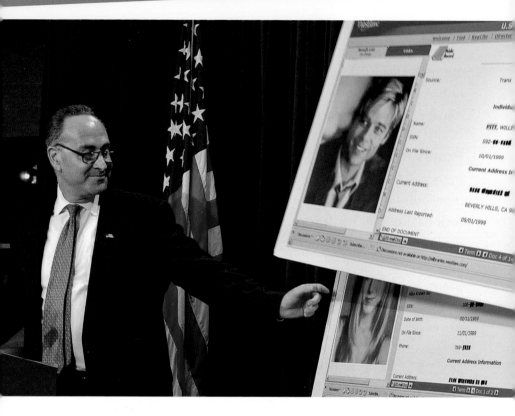

Senator Charles Schumer (D-NY) points to posters displaying personal information stolen from Brad Pitt and Jennifer Aniston, among millions of others, at a Senate committee hearing on identity theft.

and Social Security numbers to do damage. Never underestimate the creativity of someone who wants to commit a crime.

Social Networking Sites

Facebook is undoubtedly one of the most popular social networking sites on the Internet. More than 200 million people around the world maintain active profiles. Facebook makes it easy to stay in touch with friends and family through sharing pictures, status updates, and fun applications. Many users think they are sharing just with "friends," but anyone can use information on sites such as Facebook, MySpace, or Friendster to steal identities. An enterprising criminal can use information about employers, spouses, and hobbies to start taking over someone's identity.

In the context of social networking sites, people are more willing to divulge personal information, even to "friends" they may not know. Even people who are diligent about deleting spam email or not talking to strangers tend to let their guard down when using social networking sites. Downloading applications onto Facebook often grants the application creator access to a user's information, which could in turn be compromised. A young generation, open about sharing information, combined with a criminal element, often equals unprecedented ways for thieves to target victims

On social networking sites, thieves try to trick people into releasing personal information. For example, a fake bulletin circulated on MySpace asked people to click a supposed link to old school pictures. Google's social networking site, Orkut, was the target of a virus that looked for financial information. Some sites are set up to mimic the home pages of social networks and ask for user identification and password. Thieves can portray themselves as "friends" and send messages that seek to trick people into releasing their data.

Criminals can download malicious software that quickly scans social networking sites for birth dates, addresses, and names of friends. Or when scammers get people to log on to a phony site, the users' computers are infected with a virus that steals user names and passwords for a variety of sites.

Sites such as Facebook and MySpace offer users various privacy settings that control which friends can see certain information. The privacy settings generally work, but it takes time and effort to do it correctly. The various options can be confusing. Some people argue that setting privacy information should be made easier. For example, Facebook users have to navigate several different pages, and more than thirty different options, to fully protect their privacy. Under privacy settings, users can change who sees a profile,

Identity Theft Reports by State

Geographic location can determine how likely one is to become a victim of identity theft.

According to the Federal Trade Commission, Arizona, California, and Florida led the nation with the number of ID theft reports in 2008. Arizona reported 149 complaints per 100,000 people. California's rate for the same population was 139, and Florida's rate was 133. It might be safer to live in the Midwest. The states with the lowest number of identity theft reports were Iowa, North Dakota, and South Dakota, with 45, 36, and 34 complaints per 100,000 population, respectively.

The top three U.S. metropolitan areas with the highest number of complaints were Brownsville-Harlingen, Texas (with 367 complaints per 100,000 people); Napa, California (351 complaints per 100,000 people); and Madera, California (349 complaints per 100,000 people).

It is hard to know exactly why one state or city has a high number of complaints. Does more identity theft happen in those places, or are people simply more willing to report it? Experts have their theories. Identity thieves may find it easier to operate in a well-populated area where people are less likely to notice suspicious behavior. Large population centers are also attractive to criminals such as pickpockets, who can find plenty of opportunities to steal wallets and purses that may hold important financial information.

An increase in identity theft in certain areas can also be attributed to a larger elderly population, which can be more vulnerable to this type of crime. Arizona and Florida are home to many "snowbirds," retirees who move somewhere warm for the winter. More elderly people are also choosing to live year-round in these states, both in their own homes and in assisted-living facilities or nursing homes.

There is a correlation with illegal drugs, too. Places that see a lot of drug activity often find higher reports of identity theft. The two crimes can go hand-in-hand, as drug users pilfer other identities as a way to support their habits.

who can search for them, what activity shows up in their news feed, and what information is available to different applications. Officials from the site have announced plans to make it easier by having just one privacy page.

Still, it is important to remember that any information on the Internet can be taken by someone with the means and ability to get at it.

Restaurants

Many restaurants these days offer the convenience of paying at the table after a meal. While some diners pay with cash, many pay with credit cards. The server takes the credit card and runs the information through a computer out of the diner's sight. The server then returns the card and receipt to the diner, and the diner leaves after the quick transaction. Millions of these types of transactions occur each day in the United States' 935,000 restaurants, where customers spent more than $530 billion in 2007 alone.

It is no wonder that restaurants are a prime source for enterprising identity thieves. Unscrupulous servers and others with access to credit card information can easily jot down account numbers. Electronic devices make this type of crime easier than ever. A small device called a "skimmer" can swipe dozens of credit cards and store the information. A thief later downloads the information to a computer and has ready access to all the credit card numbers. In a Los Angeles case in 2007, a waitress came under suspicion when she went into the restroom after running a customer's credit card. In the restroom, she was scanning the cards through a "skimmer." It was discovered that she was part of a much larger operation in which she was paid $10 for each credit card number by another thief, who managed to rack up more than $16,000 in fraudulent charges before the scam was discovered.

"Skimming" can be hard to track. Restaurant employees involved in such crimes usually work for only a short time, such as a week—just long enough to get information to commit fraud. And people who report their credit cards as misused may never know exactly where the information theft took place.

Some restaurant chains have already implemented reforms, such as using a device that allows a card to be scanned at the table in front of the customers. Officials at Ruby Tuesday announced in 2007 that it will no longer store credit card data within its restaurants. Instead, encrypted data rather than actual credit card numbers will be sent to banks for verification.

Dozens of restaurant chains have been sued in class-action lawsuits for not using shortened versions of credit card numbers on receipts, as required by law.

Pictured here are boxes containing fraud cases cracked by the Medicaid Fraud Control Unit in New York. For every case exposed, however, there may be dozens of fraud cases that succeed, unnoticed.

2 Types of Identity Theft

IDENTITY THEFT COMES IN MANY DIFFERENT FORMS, and identity thieves commit their crimes for many different reasons. But identity crimes can be divided into a few major categories. Some of these types of identity crimes have been around for many years. Other types are fairly new. Law enforcement officials are left guessing what new types might emerge in coming years.

Financial Identity Theft

One of the most common forms of identity theft falls into the financial category. In financial identity theft, a criminal uses someone else's personal information either to use an existing account or to open a new account in the victim's name. When thieves use an existing account, this is known as "account takeover." Thieves will either add their addresses to existing accounts, or put themselves on the account as an authorized user. When thieves use information to open new accounts, they do so mostly to obtain cell phones or credit cards.

Approximately 60 percent of identity theft victims reported that the criminal used an existing credit card to commit his or her crimes. Seventeen percent of victims reported that new accounts were opened in their names.

Medical Identity Theft

With rising health-care costs in the United States, and high numbers of people without health insurance, it is not surprising that one of the fastest-growing categories of identity theft involves obtaining someone else's personal information for medical purposes. A simple visit to a doctor can cost hundreds of dollars, with medical procedures running into the thousands. Out-of-pocket costs for prescription drugs can cost hundreds or thousands of dollars a month. Health expenditures in the United States number into the trillions of dollars. A 2007 medical journal article stated that since 1992, there have been more than 19,000 reported cases of medical identity theft. The number of fraud reports grew 197 percent between 2001 and 2005.

Medical identity theft can be separated into three categories. One type of thief uses personal information to obtain health services by using the identity—and health coverage—of an insured person. Monthly health insurance premiums can be expensive if a person does not have coverage through an employer, and this type of thief may feel desperate for medical care. In the second category, medical facility personnel may be involved in an identity theft crime ring. They abuse their privacy privileges to get patient's health insurance information, and then use it to submit false bills to the insurance company or sell the health policy information to others. Health care records can be sold for $50 to $60 on the street. The third group consists of people who use others' health coverage to buy prescription drugs. These people may have a prescription drug habit themselves, or will sell the prescription drugs on the street.

Medical information is supposed to be tightly guarded. The Health Insurance Portability and Accountability Act (HIPAA) of 1996 governs who can and who cannot access someone's private medical information. In theory, individuals' private medical records are closely protected. However, HIPAA security rules can be—and are—breached. Unethical employees who have access to information can give it or sell it to anyone. But breaches of HIPAA can also happen accidentally. A stack of papers on a busy receptionist's desk can fall into the wrong hands if no one is watching.

More and more medical records are going online or are stored in computer databases, but this does not necessarily mean medical information will be more closely guarded. In early 2009, President Barack Obama pledged to get all medical records online within five years. He says it will offer more streamlined information and, more importantly, prevent medical errors that arise from sloppy paper record keeping.

More hospitals and clinics are adopting policies that require electronic medical records. The electronic records are easy to read (no messy handwriting) and can be easily transferred from facility to facility. Doctors enter personal information into a computer instead of keeping a paper file. This offers convenience for both doctors and patients. With some electronic medical records systems, patients can access their medical records over the Internet. Instead of waiting for a doctor's call or letter regarding test results, they can look them up online as soon as they are available. Patients can also be reminded to schedule upcoming tests.

But this convenience may come at a price. Identity thieves could access paper records, too, but enterprising criminals can hack into a database and in seconds acquire information on hundreds, even thousands, of people. Facilities generally encrypt data, but that does not make it free from potential attack.

In recent years, more medical facilities have hired someone called a data integrity specialist. This specialist takes a careful look at private medical information, how it is stored, and who has access to it. This careful oversight can help reduce instances of medical identity theft. Facilities that properly manage the disposal of information (properly purging outdated records from computers and shredding paper documents) lessen the risk of information falling into the wrong hands.

Criminals Target Members of the Military

As cruel as it sounds, identity thieves exploit the unique situation of military personnel to commit their crimes. A serviceman or –woman usually does not have the time to keep a close eye on credit reports or other financial statements, especially if deployed. If an identity thief obtains accounts or other information from a member of the military, it may be several months before the thief is caught. Resolving identity theft issues can compound the stress of military life.

The Department of Defense is taking steps to reduce the instances of identity theft among military personnel. For years, the military has relied solely on Social Security numbers as identifiers. But more recently, identification cards instead use a bar code or magnetic strips that contain information. The Department of Defense also educates personnel on identity theft issues and trains those in charge of data in practices that keep it safe.

Servicemen or –women on active duty can request an "active duty alert" upon a credit report. A call to just one of the credit reporting agencies is all it takes to get the alert placed on all three credit reports. This alert requires creditors to check with the account holder before issuing new lines of credit. The alert lasts for one year, but it can be lifted before that time or extended with a phone call. In addition, the account holder can designate someone to place or remove an alert in his or her absence. Still, what prevents someone else from doing this? And what if the person who removes the alert, even if designated, does so to rip off the serviceman or –woman?

Identity theft involving military personnel does happen. In 2008 a former U.S. Marine lance corporal pleaded guilty to stealing identities, including the identity of a Marine serving in Iraq. Investigators said he stole the identities of eighteen people and racked up $114,000 in purchases. Purchases included a plasma television, a computer, and a guitar.

Medical facilities have to be careful about what type of access to patient information new employees can have. A system in which one person is responsible for the entire billing process is a system that is vulnerable to fraud because no one is watching over that person's shoulder. A system of checks and balances in which many people oversee each other's work is a safer, more private system.

Trying to correct medical identity fraud can be as time-consuming as correcting financial fraud. Victims of medical identity theft often do not know that their insurance information has been stolen until they get bills for medical care they never received. Then they have to prove to the health insurer that their identity was used by someone else, correct their medical records, and sort through what can be damaging false information about their medical histories. They may find it difficult to obtain their rightful benefits or continued health insurance coverage. It can take months or even years to clear false information.

Immigration Identity Theft

Not only are identities stolen to obtain merchandise or services (such as health benefits), but sometimes they are stolen by people who want to work under a different name. In some cases, people who come to the United States without proper documentation have used alternative identities to secure employment. Often, a Social Security number of a U.S. citizen is all someone needs to get a job and assume someone else's identity in the workplace. Prosecutors say they are seeing more identity theft that falls into this category. They theorize that perhaps these cases are related to the higher number of illegal immigrants in United States.

The identity of a real person must be used in obtaining a job because many employers do background checks on employees. A background check investigates only the name and Social Security number provided; it does not verify that employees are who they say they are. An identity thief can work indefinitely as someone else as long as he or she is not caught. The Social Security Administration verifies that the number is real, but it does not check to see how many times that number is being used. One Social Security number could be used many times by many different people. In Ottawa, Kansas, for example, one woman was surprised to get a letter from the Internal Revenue Service asking for $3,300 in unpaid taxes. The taxes were related to five different jobs that the woman never did, in many different states. It turns out that her identity had been used by illegal immigrants in order to obtain work.

Uncovering this type of identity theft is difficult. Employers can face legal trouble if they hire illegal immigrants. But many say there is not much they can do to find out if their potential employees are using false names. Federal antidiscrimination laws prohibit employers from asking too many questions of applicants. That means they often have to believe that the documents they are given are real. Even if employers doubt a person is who he says he is, laws might prohibit them from inquiring further.

Those familiar with identity theft say there are many flaws in the system that allows this type of identity theft to occur. For example, the Internal Revenue Service can determine through database records who is not paying taxes, but it cannot determine who is using false identification. Even if officials suspect that a Social Security number is being used improperly, investigating identity theft is not one of the IRS's responsibilities.

Some blame the entire U.S. immigration policy. Critics say current policy makes it difficult for immigrants to come here legally. Immigrants need a visa from their home country's government, and the wait can be many years. In Mexico, immigrants who want to come to the United States legally sometimes must wait seven or more years. Those looking for the chance to make money may not feel that they can wait. As a result, they come to the United States illegally.

Perhaps another solution to this problem is to issue driver's licenses and other governmental documents to illegal immigrants.

Some believe that identity theft by immigrants is caused by our country's restrictive immigration policy. Whatever the cause, the result can ruin lives. Hector Garcia lost his job and had trouble finding another when Segundo Congache stole his identity and ran up traffic tickets and bench warrants in his name.

Already, the city of New Haven, Connecticut, gives an official ID card to illegal immigrants. In this way, the identity of the cardholder is verified. This reduces the need for someone to fake an identity to work or open bank accounts. However, critics of this plan say that it is dangerous to give illegal immigrants official government-issued documents and raises security concerns in an age marked by terrorism.

The idea of giving an identity card to all workers is being debated in Congress. Under this plan, only people authorized to work in the United States would be issued a forgery-proof card. This would make it nearly impossible for illegal immigrants to obtain work in the United States. The idea behind the card is that if illegal immigrants cannot work in the United States, they will stop coming here. Those hoping to stop the tide of illegal immigration endorse the plan. But the plan worries civil rights activists, who see the government intruding into the privacy of Americans. Activists are concerned that if the government collects data on individuals and issues cards containing that data, the information could then be used as a tool to monitor and track citizens.

Cases in which illegal immigrants use identity numbers of U.S. citizens often end up in the offices of local prosecutors. But local prosecutors are facing increased amounts of work with fewer staff because of budget cuts in the most recent economic downturn. As a result, even if convicted, illegal immigrants who use another person's identity often receive only probation. Federal, state, and local agencies do not always share information with each other, and no federal database keeps track of identity theft crimes. Only the largest and most complex identity theft crimes involving illegal immigrants end up with federal prosecutors. A 2006 Colorado investigation showed the sophistication of one such identity theft ring. According to grand jury testimony against a document-fraud ringleader, Social Security numbers and other documentation were sold for $80 to $300 on the street. The quality of documents determined the prices, with seemingly authentic driver's licenses and Social Security cards selling for the most money. The ringleader sold the documents at Laundromats and flea markets.

To what extent identity theft should be prosecuted in illegal immigration cases recently went all the way to the U.S. Supreme Court. Since 2004, federal prosecutors have been able to extend sentences of illegal immigrants if they were found to knowingly be using Social Security numbers of other people. This law was used in one of the biggest illegal immigration raids in U.S. history. In the summer of 2008 nearly four hundred illegal immigrants were arrested at a plant in Postville, Iowa. Of that number, 270 were charged with identity theft. Most of those served their sentences and were deported. In May 2009 the justices ruled unanimously that government prosecutors went too far in using identity theft laws to lengthen the jail terms of undocumented workers.

In many cases, illegal immigrants did not know they were using the Social Security number of an actual person. A randomly generated nine-digit number may—or may not—result in a number that matches another person's Social Security number. The Supreme Court justices said prosecution using the federal identity theft law relied too much on chance. If the random Social Security number was actually the real number of another person, two more years would be added to an illegal immigrant's prison sentence. But if the random number did not happen to match a real number, then the immigrant would be spared additional prison time.

Critics say that immigrants who use different identities to get jobs should not be prosecuted in the same way as other identity thieves. Some define identity theft as using another person's information in order to steal or profit. They argue that illegal immigrants are using information to find work, not gain possessions, and therefore should be treated differently.

Obtaining Disaster Benefits

When disaster strikes, identity thieves see an opportunity. Governments provide assistance for victims of natural disasters, such as floods, tornadoes, and hurricanes. Assistance includes money for shelter, food, or other necessities.

In the aftermath of Hurricane Katrina in August 2005, many thieves helped themselves to the identities of rightful disaster benefits recipients in Louisiana and Mississippi. The hurricane displaced many people from their homes in New Orleans and other nearby areas along the Gulf Coast. Residents quickly evacuated the region

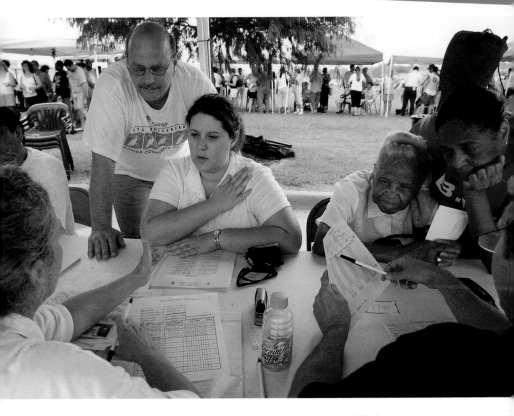

This family's home was damaged in Hurricane Katrina. They filled out insurance claims to help them cover the damage. Unfortunately, many dishonest people saw Katrina as an opportunity to pose as hurricane victims to get "free" money.

prior to the hurricane, leaving important belongings behind. In the days after the storm, while law enforcement officials were busy keeping people safe, thieves had nearly unlimited access to paperwork and other documents that had not been secured.

Almost immediately, the government realized the high possibility of fraud and created the Hurricane Katrina Fraud Task Force in September 2005 to deter thieves and investigate fraud complaints. Even years after Hurricane Katrina, victims are still finding that their personal information has been leaked. For example, in late 2008 the Federal Emergency Management Agency (FEMA) reported that nearly 17,000 names, Social Security

Consumer Trust

With more people aware of identity theft and how it occurs, it is understandable that many people have concerns about who sees their personal information and how it is used.

In early 2009 the Identity Theft Resource Center conducted a survey asking people about the perceived security of their information. Eighty-four percent of those surveyed said they were concerned about the privacy of their personal and financial information sent over the Internet. Most people said there needs to be an improvement in the way that personal information is stored in databases. Only 6 percent of those surveyed said there is little or no need for any improvement. And if businesses could find a way for people to make purchases online without providing personal information, 96 percent of respondents would be interested in learning more.

numbers, and telephone numbers of Katrina victims were posted to two public websites. The information was removed as soon as FEMA officials discovered the posts. Also in 2008, a government mailing subcontractor sent letters with personal information in mistakenly addressed envelopes. This mistake affected about a thousand people. In that case, FEMA offered identity theft monitoring to all those affected.

Identity theft experts urge people in disaster-prone areas to keep important personal documents in a locked box. Copies should be stored together so they're easy to grab in case of emergency or evacuation. During the chaos in the wake of a disaster, victims often need official documents to jump-start the insurance claim and benefits process. Victims who are carrying personal documents with them should keep track of them at all times. An identity thief may be lurking anywhere, and often will strike when people are at their most vulnerable.

Funding Terrorist Activities

A big concern in the aftermath of the September 11, 2001, attacks is people using false names to perpetrate criminal activity that results in terrorism.

What may seem like an ordinary criminal identity theft case may actually lead federal investigators to terrorist cells. Terrorists have used identity theft to obtain employment in someone else's name and to gain access to secure areas. An Al-Qaeda terrorist cell in Spain used stolen credit cards to make purchases needed for terrorist activities. The stolen credit cards, along with stolen telephone cards, were used to communicate with other members of the organization in the Middle East. False passports and other travel documents were used to open bank accounts that supported terrorist activities.

Automated teller machines (ATMs) are prime—and surprisingly easy—targets for identity thieves.

3 How Identity Theft Occurs

IDENTITY THEFT CAN OCCUR IN COUNTLESS WAYS. Every day, thieves come up with new scams and new uses of technology to commit their crimes. It is difficult to stay on top of all the new schemes and scams. However, there are some standard methods that thieves use again and again to gain access to people's identities. Unfortunately, they are used over and over because they work. These methods include tricking people into revealing information, stealing information, or using high-tech methods to gain access to information. The more that people become aware of the ways in which identity thieves commit their crimes, the more likely identity theft can be slowed or even stopped.

Common Scams

Identity thieves will often trick people into revealing personal information. These thieves do not need to steal wallets or purses. They simply persuade victims to give out account information, birth dates, and the like. They rely upon a few tried-and-true scams to obtain identities and then start committing fraud and other crimes.

The Phony Bank Examiner

This scam operates over the telephone. Someone calls and says he or she is an official at the bank where the victim has an account. The caller says there has been a problem at the bank and asks the victim to verify information such as account numbers, recent activity, or balances. The caller also tries to determine whether the person lives alone or is otherwise vulnerable to a scam. He or she says another bank official will be in touch with more information.

Sometime later that day, the victim will get another call. This one is from a person claiming to be a bank examiner. The bank examiner says that a dishonest teller is stealing money. The victim is asked to withdraw a large sum of money and deposit it into another account in hopes of catching the fictitious teller. The victim is told that the money is fully insured and that nothing will happen to it. But in reality the account is set up in the thief's name. Sometimes the callers even go so far as to meet with the victims and produce phony receipts that show the transactions.

Helpful hint: People should be aware that in a real bank investigation, account holders' actual money is never used. Anyone claiming to be a bank official should show proof of identity. In a situation like this, it is best to call the bank to find out if indeed there are any problems.

Rigged ATMs

Automated teller machines (ATMs) certainly make life easier for many people. The machines allow quick and convenient access to cash anywhere, anytime. People do not hesitate to swipe a card and punch a few keys in order for the machine to spit out money. But anywhere there is money, there are thieves hoping to profit.

Thieves use a variety of methods to steal information from ATMs. For example, they can attach wireless devices that are engineered to gather card numbers and PIN information. The devices mimic real ATM card slots. They are hard to detect, and most people cannot tell that they are not using a legitimate ATM. Thieves may be waiting nearby as their device reads the account numbers wirelessly. They also can aim a tiny camera at the keypad so they can capture PINs. Thieves then load the numbers onto blank cards.

Another way to steal PINs is to place a thin keypad over the original keypad. This way, thieves can record the numbers that victims punch in. Again, this phony keypad can be hard for the average person to detect.

Identity thieves generally will rig several ATMs in one area. They most often strike during weekends and holidays for two reasons: one, the ATMs are busier because people generally withdraw more cash during these times and two, banks are closed and thieves can swipe a large amount of money before the victims can notify their banks and close an account.

Helpful hint: Be aware of any ATM that looks strange. The card slot may be cracked, or the screen may display odd instructions. Always shield the keypad in case a small camera is mounted somewhere nearby. Try to use ATMs that are operated by a bank instead of a private individual or company.

Card Verification

This is another scam done over the telephone. Callers use many scenarios to try to get victims to reveal credit card information. For example, a caller might say he is calling from a credit card company to investigate fraudulent charges, and he needs a credit card number and expiration date to aid in the investigation. Or a caller may pose as an online merchant and say she needs to verify card information for payment. Once a thief has a card number, an expiration date, and the smaller verification number on the back, he or she can start racking up charges.

Helpful hint: Never give out credit card information when prompted by a caller. The only time people should reveal account information over the phone or online is when they have originated the contact.

Economic Downturn and Identity Theft

The economic downturn that began in 2008 provided more motivation for identity thieves. In times of desperation and financial worry, authorities report that more people are turning toward schemes and crimes to obtain money and goods. Some experts believe that in this economy, we will see more small-scale identity thieves in addition to the larger, well-organized crime rings.

The same financial fears that make some people commit crimes can make other people more vulnerable to these thieves. The schemers take advantage of people's economic worries. For example, a phishing scheme may claim to offer a good deal to get out of a financial crisis. But in reality, the "deal" is just a way for the thief to fraudulently obtain personal information.

One business that has not been affected by the sagging economy is the criminal business of selling personal and account information on the street. Thieves are still charging about $30 for credit card information, and bank account numbers can be bought at prices ranging from $10 to $1,000.

In these times, fewer people have the resources to weather an identity theft attack. The economy has devalued investments and safety nets, money that had been saved to get through difficult times.

Census Count
and Identity
Theft

With increased awareness of identity theft, the good news is that more people are warier about sharing personal information. This posed a problem for 2010 U.S. Census Bureau workers, who in early 2009 were canvassing neighborhoods to verify addresses. Workers needed the correct addresses to send out census questionnaires in early 2010. Many workers reported that people were less willing to give out information, even when it was just an address. Some of this wariness was understandable, because identity thieves have been known to pose as census workers to obtain Social Security numbers and other data from trusting victims.

Legitimate U.S. Census workers never ask for Social Security numbers or any financial information. The workers wear badges and carry handheld computers with them. They will provide, if asked, a phone number of a supervisor. In addition, U.S. Census workers take an oath in which they pledge not to reveal personal data to anyone. Violation of that oath can result in a $250,000 fine or five years in jail.

Lottery Claims

Some victims receive a call, letter, or email that says they have won a lottery in a foreign country. The scammer claims that before the payment can be processed, the officials need personal information such as full name, date of birth, telephone number, and an account number at a bank where the money can (supposedly) be transferred.

Helpful hint: Disregard any notices that claim lottery winnings. In order to win a lottery, people have to buy a ticket or register for a drawing. People are not randomly chosen to win money.

False Charities

It is human nature to want to help those who are less fortunate. Unfortunately, identity thieves take advantage of this compassion by soliciting money for phony charities. A caller will claim she works for a charity that is looking for donations, then ask for a credit card number and expiration date. Because so many legitimate charities ask for donations by phone, it can be difficult to distinguish what is real from what is not. Thieves prey upon people at the most unsuspecting times. After the 9/11 terrorist attacks, many victims were duped into providing personal information by hustlers calling and requesting money for a 9/11 victims' fund that did not exist.

Helpful hint: Before donating through an unsolicited request, take time to check out the charity. Most states require that charities register with the attorney general's office. A legitimate charity will have a way to donate securely over the Internet, and its website will have easy-to-find phone numbers and emails of staff members who can respond to inquiries.

Fake Invoices

In this scam, victims receive counterfeit (but authentic-looking) invoices either through regular mail or email. The invoice states that the victim bought something, and now the payment is due. Elderly people can be especially vulnerable to this scam because they may think that they may have forgotten to pay for an item. Thieves use the invoice to try to get victims to pay with a credit card or check, the account numbers of which will subsequently be stolen.

Helpful hint: These invoices usually do not include a telephone number. Real businesses always include a telephone number and other contact information. When there is a phone number included in an invoice, people should always call to verify an invoice before sending money.

Phony Brokerage Firms

In this scam, victims receive an email reporting a "hot stock tip." For details, he or she must click on the web link provided. This takes the victim to a website that appears to represent a legitimate stock brokerage firm. To receive more information, the victim is asked to provide confidential financial information.

Helpful hint: Legitimate brokerage companies will not solicit stock buys through an email. Always check with a real broker to see if the tip is legitimate. A live person will have the best advice on what types of stocks to buy.

Temporary Account Suspension

Here, victims get a phone call or email that says an account has been suspended. The thief says that the bank is reviewing all accounts to check for fraud, and the victim must provide account information in order for the review to take place. Victims are asked for names, birth dates, account numbers, and PINs. If the information is not provided, victims are told, their account will be canceled.

Helpful hint: Again, do not provide financial and personal information that is solicited from a stranger. A bank would never close someone's account because he or she failed to provide personal information.

Money Mule Schemes

In today's economy, more people may be vulnerable to offers of easy and quick employment. A money mule scheme falls into this category. A person—the "mule" (which takes its name from a person who transports drugs)—may get an offer via phone, email, or a website for a job as a financial manager or payment processor. A money mule is asked to open an account into which sums of money will be deposited. The person with the account is told he or she can keep a certain percentage, such as 10 percent. The person must forward the rest of the money to a different account.

What is really happening is that the money involved has been stolen, often through identity theft. The "employer" wants the money to come through an innocent account so it cannot be tracked. This is an illegal act of money laundering, and the "employee" is participating in the crime. In addition, the "employee" is likely to be the "employer's" next identity theft victim, having provided account information and perhaps other personal information.

False Voting Registries

It happens every election year: Criminals go door-to-door, claiming that they work for an organization that registers people to vote. In this way, they are able to obtain personal information from many people in a short amount of time.

Helpful hint: Always ask for the organization's main phone number so you can call to verify the identities of people asking for your information. If these people are working for a legitimate group, they will be happy to provide you with contact information.

High-Tech Dangers

While identity theft has always been a concern, there's no question that technology such as computers, online banking, and other high-tech devices—such as cell phones—have made it easier than ever for thieves to snatch personal information. Consumers need to be aware that their everyday habits on computers or cell phones could result in identity theft. While people cannot be expected to unplug from these modern conveniences, there are ways to reduce identity theft risk when using technology. The first step is to become aware of the dangers, and then take action to lessen those dangers.

A recent survey by *Consumer Reports* National Research Center found that one in five online consumers were the victim of a "cybercrime." Most of those crimes involved the theft of personal information. The same survey, released in May 2009, reported that 1.7 million households were victims of computer identity theft in the past year.

The following are some high-tech traps thieves use to capture personal and financial information.

Spyware

Throughout the world, people install programs that can look into computer browsers, view the sites people are visiting, and extract personal information that is entered into those sites, such as names, addresses, and billing information. These programs are known as spyware, because they spy on private information. Spyware can be physically installed on a computer, or it can be remotely installed via the Internet. Sometimes a victim has actually agreed to the remote spyware installation by clicking "I agree" on one of those long user agreements found during software installation. Few people read the fine print, which may include information about spyware.

File sharing also puts computers at risk for spyware monitoring. File sharing users agree to download software that connects their computers to a network of other users. This makes it easy to share games, music, and movies. But it also makes it easier for thieves to tap into a vast network of computers and install spyware that tracks personal information.

Marion Carnegie Library
206 S. Market St
Marion. IL 62959

People often download spyware without realizing they have done so. This Gentry Mullen illustration shows a person furious over spyware having invaded the computer.

Besides simply looking for personal information, some spyware can monitor keystrokes. When a person types in a user name and password, those keystrokes are noted and saved. Keystroke spyware makes it easy for someone to obtain user names and passwords to get into otherwise-secure accounts.

Most often, these types of programs are unknowingly downloaded. Spyware lurks in email invitations and web advertisements.

Helpful hint: Do not download even innocent-looking programs from unknown sources. Email attachments, links, and web page advertisements are common hiding places used by people trying to infect other computers with spyware. Even a harmless-looking program could contain spyware that results in identity theft. If more people avoided clicking on suspicious email invitations or web advertisements, spyware would have a more difficult time finding a home.

Wi-Fi Networks

These days, anyone can take a laptop computer almost anywhere and connect to the Internet through wireless networks (often free of charge). People who work on computers are no longer tethered to modem cables, so coffee shops, restaurants, and parks are becoming alternate work spaces. The freedom to move around is appealing, but that freedom is also tinged with danger.

In wireless networks, web-page information is sent over radio waves. Hackers can find ways to tap into unprotected wireless networks and grab the information that is being sent. User names, passwords, and account information is vulnerable. Wireless routers typically have a range of five hundred feet or more. That means a household's wireless network can be tapped into from a neighbor's house or from the street. It is not uncommon for thieves to drive through the streets with their laptops, checking for unsecured networks.

Network providers are coming up with better security options for customers. For example, Verizon allows wireless network users to install their own encryption if they are linked into an unencrypted network (which often happens in wireless "hot spots" or public places).

Protection hint: Only use networks that are secure. Homes and businesses should always have password-protected wireless networks. Give passwords only to trusted people. At home, most routers have an "invisible" option, which prevents other people from seeing a wireless network. If an unsecured network must be used, be sure not to visit websites that contain personal or financial information, such as banks or other financial institutions. Do not buy items with a credit card on the Internet on unsecured networks.

Phishing

Identity thieves often go "phishing" for information. This means that identity thieves troll the waters of the Internet, hoping to lure someone into giving up personal information, such as user names, passwords, or account numbers.

For example, a scammer will send a legitimate-looking email to an unsuspecting victim. The email claims to be from a bank, financial institution, or any company that holds account information. The email may say something like "an account is out-of-date and information needs to be re-entered and verified." Victims are told to either respond to the email or click on a link to to a website and enter their information. The phony website often looks so real that victims trust the request. But a thief lurks behind the email or website, waiting to collect the sensitive personal information and use it for his or her own purposes. At any one time, there are tens of thousands of phishing sites in operation.

Banks are fighting phishing scams on their own terms. Most often, when a financial institution obtains knowledge of a phishing scam that directs customers to a phony website, officials will ask Internet service providers to shut down the site. In October 2008 one company, Bank of America, began taking this one step further. Instead of simply shutting down the phishing site, the Internet service provider was instructed to redirect people to an informational page created by the bank. This page tells customers that they were lured to a phony site by a phishing scam and almost became victims of identity theft. It gives information on how to avoid this type of fraud in the future. Seven months after the program went

Phishy Beginnings

Phishing is a relatively new technique that came about in the first days of widespread Internet use. Before 2003 phishing was rather unsophisticated. Phishing traps came in the form of emails, usually rife with spelling and grammatical errors that called attention to the illegitimacy of the claims. It did not take long for the criminals to realize that if they were savvier, they could trap more unsuspecting people. They began setting up websites that looked like the sites of legitimate companies, such as Yahoo! and eBay. "Customers" were sent emails with links to these fraudulent websites. The operations became more sophisticated, with software programs that hide the scammers' URLs by covering them with floating windows that appear to display the legitimate URLs.

Individual states are stepping up prosecution of the people behind phishing schemes. For example, violation of Illinois's Anti-Phishing Act can result in up to a $500,000 fine.

into effect, more than 70,000 people had been redirected to the educational page. Plans are in place to translate the page into more than twenty languages so it can be used around the world.

Each spring, around tax time, scammers send out emails that look as if they come from the Internal Revenue Service. The email may ask the recipient to supply personal information in order to receive a tax refund. The real IRS communicates with people only through the U.S. postal service. However, because these types of scams are so common, the IRS has an email account to report such crimes: phishing@irs.gov.

In recent years, banking regulators have required that institutions with online banking offerings take an extra step in guarding against phishing. Not only do customers log in with a user name and password, but an image chosen by the customer (such as a bird or television set) is also displayed on the screen. This image lets customers know that they are using the bank's authentic site, and not a "dummy" one.

The number of phishing websites continues to increase. A study done by the Anti-Phishing Working Group found that the number of sites jumped an incredible 827 percent from January to December 2008. The number of sites designed to steal passwords and other information totaled just more than 31,000 at the end of 2008. A *Consumer Reports* survey found that phishing attacks were successful in 1 in 13 households with Internet access.

With more people using cell phones, identity thieves are finding new ways to obtain personal information. Scammers now use phishing text messages in much the same way as they have been using phishing emails. Victims receive a text message claiming to be from a bank or other financial institution. The message asks the victim to respond and verify personal information. One such scam occurred in Jackson County, Florida, in February 2009. Consumers should be aware that real banks and financial institutions will not ask for personal information via emails or text messages.

Helpful hint: Just as over the telephone, never give out account information when solicited by a stranger. Always verify that emails and websites are legitimate. Call the bank or financial institution to verify any requests concerning accounts.

Other High-Tech Dangers

Each year, better and more advanced technology is available at our fingertips. As technology improves, new devices are able to store more information in a smaller space. This means that devices such as digital cameras and cell phone cameras are not only more sophisticated but also easier to hide. As a result, a thief can snap a picture of a credit card or take a short video of someone punching in a PIN on an ATM machine without a victim even realizing it. That's why it is important to always be aware of surroundings and be wary of people who may be watching and waiting to capture sensitive data.

Social Engineering

Some identity thieves need minimal information before striking. People may think they are safe from identity thieves because they do not share Social Security numbers or account information. But these same people may not think twice about sharing others types of personal information. Savvy identity thieves use a tactic called social engineering to get people to reveal seemingly innocent information. Then they use these facts as the key to unlock bigger, more useful data.

For example, many people use a pet's name or a child's name or birth date as a password or PIN. Identity thieves with this information can try to hack into a person's account. In another form of social engineering, criminals approach banks and other institutions posing as actual customers. They try to get tellers and other employees to give out account information.

People should be very careful not to reveal any type of personal information. Identity thieves will try to use anything to commit their crimes. Banks and other financial institutions should always ask for verification of someone's identity before revealing account information or performing any transactions.

How to Protect Yourself

Computers hold a variety of sensitive information, but there are steps to take to lessen the risk of identity theft through a computer.

- Try to get rid of personal and financial information as soon as possible. For example, a tax return prepared on a computer should be printed or saved to a disk or flash drive, then erased from the computer's hard drive as soon as the return has been filed.
- Invest in an antivirus program, or obtain one of the many free antivirus programs available on the Internet. Keep it updated. This prevents harmful spyware from infecting a computer.
- Install a firewall. Firewalls make it more difficult for hackers to obtain information stored on a computer.
- When selling or otherwise getting rid of an old computer, make sure all information is permanently erased. Deleted information often can remain on a hard drive. Use a program that is designed to wipe information from a computer.
- Install all updates and patches provided by the computer's manufacturer or operating system manufacturer. Microsoft, for example, provides security-related updates through its site: www.microsoft.com/en/us/default.aspx

Some of these scams seem so ridiculous that it is hard to believe people would fall for them. But every year, thieves obtain thousands and thousands of names and account information from these types of scams. Many identity thieves know how to make themselves sound official or produce official-looking documents. Thieves also prey on fear—fear that an account is closed, or fear that a teller is dishonest and will steal a victim's money. Claims that a person has won money also appeal to many victims' desire for riches. But remember the old saying: if it seems too good to be true, it probably is.

This stereotypical image of a masked thief vanishing into the night is belied by the reality that identity thieves are often friends or relatives of their victims.

4 Issues Surrounding Identity Theft

AT FIRST GLANCE, THE ISSUE OF IDENTITY THEFT
appears simplistic: Identity thief targets victim. Victim loses money
and security. Identity thief, if caught, pays the price. But upon
further examination, a broader picture emerges. Issues to consider
include the following: Who is perpetrating the crimes, and why?
Why do experts believe these crimes are underreported? What role
does and should law enforcement play? Who ultimately pays the
price when identity theft is discovered?

Identity Thieves

Identity thieves are not always mysterious, shadowy criminals hiding behind computer screens. They can be relatives, friends, or
next-door neighbors. They can be old or young. They can be the
nicest man or woman on the block. They do not walk around advertising their crimes. It is impossible to recognize an identity thief
on the streets. Some of the rationalizations behind their actions can
be surprising.

Supporting a habit. The demand for cash to fuel alcohol, drug,
or gambling addiction can drive someone to use identity theft
to obtain money in illegal ways. An addict may already be used to
avoiding the law and may decide there is no risk in compounding
the problem. Addiction can cloud judgment, causing someone to
take actions that he or she would not otherwise take.

Justifying the behavior. Perhaps an identity thief is using someone else's money to get out of a serious jam. It could be a single mother in danger of losing her home. It could be a son who needs to buy expensive medicine for a parent. They may feel they have nowhere else to turn, and that the greater good outweighs their illegal actions.

Feeling entitled. Evidence of living well is apparent in every aspect of today's society. Luxury cars speed down roadways. Grand houses pop up in new developments. Private schools offer exclusive educations to children. People accustomed to extravagant lifestyles may find themselves down on their luck. Instead of admitting the downturn, these people may decide to find a way to continue to live well. The pressure to keep up with neighbors can cause individuals to make poor choices.

Obtaining work. Identity theft does not always result in financial fraud. Some people use a false identity to obtain work. They may be illegal immigrants. Perhaps they want to hide a checkered employment history. More employers are requesting credit checks and not hiring people who have had financial problems. An employee may think that working under someone else's identity is the only way to get a job.

When Friends or Family Members Are the Criminals

The majority of identity theft crimes are perpetrated by strangers. The victims may never find out who used their identities. But occasionally, friends and family members are the identity thieves. People in desperate financial situations may seize the opportunity to obtain a friend or relative's personal information. Unfortunately, it is easy for identity thieves to abuse the trust common among friends and relatives. It is not difficult to slip a credit card from a wallet, to take a blank check or a Social Security card when someone is not looking. Friends and relatives may be privy to personal information such as birth dates and maiden names that are used to verify accounts.

One thing is certain: an identity thief who turns out to be a friend or relative complicates the situation. There are many factors that victims need to take into consideration. How best to resolve the situation becomes a very personal decision.

According to a Federal Trade Commission survey, 16 percent of identity theft victims said they knew the thief. This might be a neighbor, relative, friend, coworker, or in-home employee.

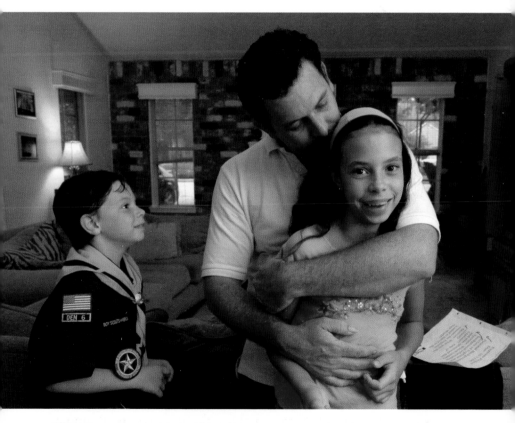

The expression "you always hurt the one you love" takes on new meaning in identity theft cases perpetrated by family members. Eric Wagenhauser of Texas discovered that his ex-wife had used their children's Social Security numbers to apply for credit cards.

Emotional
Impact

Identity theft victims often find themselves experiencing many different emotions as they try to resolve their cases. It is important to acknowledge the emotions and talk about them before they spiral out of control. Victims should speak to a trusted friend or relative about their situation and how they are addressing the problem. Other people can provide support and feedback during a victim's sensitive time.

When identity theft is first discovered, common emotions include surprise, embarrassment, and the feeling of being alone. Then, after working to resolve the issue, victims may feel overwhelmed and frustrated. Resolving identity theft requires much paperwork, time, energy, and sometimes money. Phone calls and letters may go unanswered, and victims might be shuttled from one voicemail to another. It may seem like the problem will never end.

Then there is the feeling of insecurity and mistrust. It is hard to feel secure when someone has stolen personal information that is supposed to be confidential. And if the thief was a relative or friend, it can be hard to develop trusting relationships again.

Those in financial charge of a household may experience feelings of guilt and powerlessness. Identity theft can destroy credit ratings, making it difficult to purchase a house or a car. Identity theft can completely change a family's routine and way of life. Achieving certain financial dreams may be delayed.

There are many ways to take control of the situation. Acknowledging the emotions is an important first step. Staying organized and on-task can help victims regain a sense of control. It is also important not to let the crime absorb all of one's time. Take time to go out for dinner, catch a movie, or exercise. Some victims find purpose in becoming advocates for identity theft awareness. They may join support groups or work on behalf of laws that assist victims or protect potential victims.

If the problem still seems overwhelming, it might be time to speak with a professional counselor, especially one who specializes in treating crime victims.

Personally knowing the identity thief can make a difficult situation even harder. Many victims are reluctant to press charges or file a police report, especially if the thief is a close relative. Victims do not want to see their son or their mother thrown in jail. But officials at the Identity Theft Resource Center make it clear that the victim is not responsible for the jail time or criminal charges; the thief brought it upon himself or herself by committing the crime.

Victims can make several choices when dealing with an identity thief they know. For one, they can treat this crime like any other and file a police report. Without a police report, it can be difficult to prove to creditors and credit bureaus that an identity theft has actually occurred.

A way to resolve the situation without criminal action is to hire a mediator. Mediation works when all parties are in agreement. A mediator will help both victim and criminal reach an agreement on how outstanding bills can be paid. The agreement is legally binding.

If victims are reluctant to file charges against a relative or friend, they can contact creditors to see if the situation can be resolved without police involvement. This usually demands the cooperation of both victim and criminal. Sometimes a creditor can be persuaded to transfer the bill to the identity thief. This will require a statement signed by the thief and sent to the creditor.

Some victims decide to do nothing and settle the debt themselves. Victims will choose this route if they want to protect the identity thief and give him or her another chance. In other cases, family members or other friends will pressure the victim into forgiving the situation. They may offer to help the victim pay off the debt, or they may work out a deal with the identity thief in which the thief agrees to pay off the debt. Victims should be aware that if they pay off the debt themselves, the poor credit reports and ratings remain in their name. Choosing this route will not fix bad credit. Filing a police report is the only way to clear fraudulent credit records.

Famous Identity Theft Cases

It is no surprise that identity theft cases involving celebrities or outrageous actions can dominate national headlines.

One of the most famous identity theft cases involves a man named Frank Abagnale Jr.

Frank Abagnale, portrayed by Leonardo DiCaprio in the movie *Catch Me If You Can*, can be said to have "invented" identity theft. During the 1960s Abagnale, who did not go to college, successfully posed as an airline pilot and a doctor among other vocations, successfully scamming $2 million before he was caught. Once out of prison, he went to work helping the government identify those who commit identity theft and other types of fraud.

In the 1960s, the young Abagnale assumed a variety of identities, including an airline pilot and a doctor, successfully forging payroll checks and scamming more than $2 million through fraud in every state. Abagnale primarily used check forgery as a means of stealing the identities of others, and he impersonated his victims as well. After the FBI caught up with Abagnale, he helped the agency find others who were also using identity theft scams. Abagnale's story was made into a critically acclaimed 2002 film, *Catch Me If You Can*, starring Leonardo DiCaprio as Abagnale and Tom Hanks as an FBI agent. Today, Abagnale continues to work with the government in identifying fraud cases and speaks to businesses and organizations around the country on topics related to fraud.

In another case, in New York City in 2001, Abraham Abdallah was charged with criminal impersonation, forgery, and fraud for allegedly using the personal information of celebrities and other wealthy individuals. Court documents say that Abdallah, a restaurant busboy, used a copy of *Forbes* magazine, the Internet, and cell phones to obtain Social Security numbers, credit card numbers, and financial records. When he tried to transfer $10 million from a top executive's brokerage account, company officials became suspicious and authorities were alerted. Authorities think that Abdallah may have obtained the personal information of stars including Steven Spielberg, Oprah Winfrey, Martha Stewart, and Ted Turner.

In the early 1990s, a man named James Rinaldo Jackson managed to compile personal information of dozens of Hollywood stars and Wall Street bankers. He acquired Steven Spielberg's credit card records. He got personal and financial information regarding Mel Gibson and Danny DeVito. Perhaps most shocking, he was able to compile this information using a phone from inside a prison. All it took was one leak to open the door for Jackson. He started by finding out the name of the Screen Actors Guild medical provider. Then he called the provider and, pretending to be an administrator looking to verify medical bills, received the Social Security number, address, and date of birth for Steven Spielberg. Accomplices helped him cover up his frequent phone calls from the prison phone, but eventually he was caught. Jackson, like Abagnale, now travels the world, giving talks on how people can avoid the same type of scams he perpetrated.

In April 2009 an actor on the television series *One Tree Hill* was charged with selling Social Security numbers and cards. U.S. Immigration and Customs Enforcement officials caught Antwon Tanner, age thirty-five, selling the numbers over the phone. Tanner had also appeared in the movie *Coach Carter* and on TV shows such as *Boston Legal* and *CSI*. An informant tipped off an undercover agent, who ended up buying sixteen Social Security numbers and three falsified cards for $10,000 from the actor. It was not clear how the numbers had been obtained or how they were planned to be used.

In January 2010 Tanner pleaded guilty in a federal courtroom in Brooklyn. He was sentenced to three months in prison and five months of house arrest.

Much identity theft is the work of organized groups of criminals. The Spanish government uncovered an arsenal of weapons that had been stolen by criminals involved in identity theft and robberies.

Organized Crime Rings

In a more sophisticated twist on identity theft, thieves band together to form crime rings to defraud people and governments of millions of dollars. These crime rings can be well organized and well hidden, often involving people based in several countries. They often use sophisticated technology to commit their crimes. In August 2009 U.S. officials busted an identity theft crime ring based in the United States and Israel. Crime ring members allegedly used the identities of federal prisoners to file tax returns and claim tax refunds, without the prisoners' knowledge. The money was deposited in Israeli bank accounts. The suspects had hoped to get more than $35 million.

The Reporting Process

Documenting identity theft and clearing a good name takes time, effort, and often money. Victims are urged to contact their local law enforcement agency to file an official report. But it is here that frustration can take hold. The Identity Theft Resource Center reports that some of the most frequent complaints from victims center on lack of law enforcement response. Victims often feel that law enforcement officials do not regard identity theft as a serious enough crime to warrant staff time and investigation. Or, if law enforcement does respond, victims may think officers are not acting fast enough or doing enough to catch the criminals. The truth of the matter is that many identity thieves are never caught. By the time their crimes are detected, they may have moved on. Or perhaps they were using public computers to perpetrate their crimes and cannot be traced. In any case, though, victims want to feel as if law enforcement is helping them.

Sometimes, law enforcement agencies do not have the time to fully investigate or solve the crime. Many law enforcement agencies, especially at local levels, are short-staffed and devote their energy to crimes of violence such as assault, kidnapping, and homicide. However, it benefits law enforcement agencies to follow up on all reports of identity theft because the investigation may uncover larger, more serious crimes. Thieves often use false identities to deal drugs, evade arrest, and commit fraud.

One study of law enforcement and identity theft showed that officers estimate that only 11 percent of all identity theft cases are solved. Identity theft cases can become complicated for many reasons. First is the fact that some of the crimes occur across city, county, or state lines. If the victim and criminal live in different areas, it is not clear in which jurisdiction the report should be filed. Second, the thief often does not use his or her real name, making him or her difficult to track. Third, information comes from many different sources (victim, financial institution, credit agency, etc.) and can be time-consuming to track.

Because identity thieves often cross through different jurisdictions, it is important for law enforcement officials to track criminals on the move. Different agencies need ways to share identity theft cases with one another.

The Consumer Sentinel ID Theft Data Clearinghouse holds nearly 300,000 identity theft complaints from around the nation. Law enforcement officials can use the database to look for connections among different cases. Use of the database may lead to the discovery of larger identity theft crime rings.

In July 2008 the U.S. attorney in the eastern district of Pennsylvania announced the creation of the National Identity Crime Law Enforcement network (NICLE). Data collected from law enforcement agencies regarding identity theft will be uploaded to a central computer network. Officers can find out if a particular driver's license or credit card has been used in different locations, thus tying crimes together. Agencies across the country have access to the database.

Of course, any time governmental agencies collect personal data, there is a risk of privacy invasion. Civil libertarians—people concerned about privacy rights—worry that information stored in such a database can be used for the wrong purposes. Perhaps an innocent person's information ends up in the database, and as a result, he or she is targeted by police. Do the benefits outweigh the risk? For every one hundred identity thieves caught because of such a database, is it all right if one innocent person is mistakenly targeted?

Underreporting Identity Theft

There are many indications that identity theft is underreported. In 2005 the Federal Trade Commission estimated that as many as 10 million people were victims of identity theft. However, the number of official complaints filed with the FTC was about

250,000. And of those, only 100,000 reported the information to law enforcement officials.

So why are these crimes so underreported? For one thing, law enforcement personnel in some states do not even take identity theft reports. Or if they do, they don't investigate the matter. Victims may feel that no one is willing to help them, so why should they even bother reporting it? It also can be difficult to determine which jurisdiction should handle the complaint. So much identity theft occurs across state lines. Does the victim's local police department have jurisdiction? Or should law enforcement officials where the criminal lives take charge? This type of

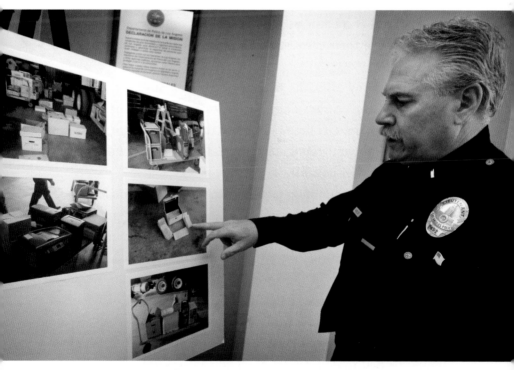

Lieutenant Rick Angelos of the Los Angeles Police Department described a series of raids on an identity theft crime ring responsible for millions of dollars in fraudulent criminal activity. The raids were achieved through cooperation among a number of different agencies, which formed a task force to combat these crimes.

confusion can inhibit victims from filing complaints. Victims can also be deterred by the anonymity of the crime. By the time the crime is discovered, the thief may have moved on to someone else. He or she may have used a public computer to commit crimes, making it even more difficult and time-consuming to track. In some cases, finding the criminal can be impossible.

Whose Responsibility?

Unlike other crimes, in which law enforcement officials take on the burden of investigation, identity theft is a crime in which the victims bear most of the responsibility for documenting the crimes. Already stressed by the discovery of the crimes, victims have the added ordeal of spending time, money, and other resources on trying to resolve their cases. Victims must often become their own advocates.

But in many cases, the victims are in the best position to show evidence of the crimes. They have the documents that show the fraudulent charges. It becomes important that the victim takes an active role in investigating the fraud and assisting law enforcement officials whenever possible.

Further compounding stresses are the lack of penalties criminals can receive if caught. In many states, the amount of prison time is tied to the amount of money obtained through identity theft. For example, in Florida the crime becomes categorized as a more serious penalty only if the amount stolen is more than $75,000. Anything less than that is regarded as a misdemeanor, which may result in spending a few days or weeks in prison, if at all, versus months or years in prison for a felony. Many wonder if penalties should be tied to dollar amounts. Did someone who lost $74,999 suffer less than a person who lost $75,000? That is what the different penalties seem to indicate.

5 Preventing Identity Theft

THE INCREASE IN IDENTITY THEFT HAS ONE BENEFIT: more people are now aware of this crime and are taking steps to prevent it. Preventive measures put in place today may result in a safer world tomorrow. Individuals, businesses, and the government are working to reduce the risk of identity theft. Routine practices of years past, especially in terms of sharing personal information, are being cast aside in favor of more secure measures. Individuals realize there are safety measures they can take. There are even companies that, for a fee, will monitor people's credit and help safeguard their identities. But paying for these services raises some important questions.

Businesses are interested in protecting their customers, so they are taking steps to make databases more secure. And the government has put laws into place that both criminalize identity theft and make it easier for consumers to keep track of their credit and to report crimes. But some of these laws, especially in terms of data-gathering and ease of understanding, are not without controversy.

Individuals

People can reduce their risk of being identity theft victims by staying alert, acting smart, and not divulging personal information. It is possible to stay safe at home, in public, and online. Smart practices can lead to increased safety and increased protection of one's identity.

At Home

Even though many identity thieves use the anonymity and ease of the Internet to commit their crimes, plenty of criminals still go about their crimes the old-fashioned way: by rifling through people's mail and trash.

If possible, use a locked mailbox, either at the curb or at a post office. Avoid placing outgoing mail in an unsecured curb mailbox. Instead, take it directly to a post office collection box. Retrieve mail as soon as possible. Avoid letting it sit in an unsecured mailbox for any length of time. Shred credit card offers or other such documents before placing them in the trash or recycling bin. When moving, fill out a change of address form well in advance of the move.

Document shredding companies have grown significantly in size in the last ten or so years now that identity theft has become such a pressing concern.

Shredder Sales

It is no surprise that the paper-shredder industry has seen a surge in the number of people buying equipment to dispose of sensitive information. In recent years, with more attention given to identity theft, more people know the importance of shredding documents containing account numbers, names, birth dates, Social Security numbers, and the like.

In 2003 office retailers such as Office Max and Staples reported a surge of 30 percent and 50 percent, respectively, in shredder sales.

Shredders are easy to obtain, and price variations can fit almost any budget. A simple strip-cut shredder can cost as little as $10. A cross-cut model that shreds documents both vertically and horizontally (which identity theft experts recommend) start at about $30, while shredders that can destroy credit cards can sell for less than $40. Larger industrial models used at businesses can cost hundreds of dollars.

Businesses are required by law under FACTA to shred documents containing employee information. Even people who employ just one person must shred all documents—not simply throw them away—that are related to the employee.

People without shredders who still want to eliminate certain documents can attend one of many "shred days" held around the country. During "shred days," consumers can bring bags or boxes of documents to a communal shredder. The events typically occur soon after the April 15 tax deadline, a time of year when taxpayers have gathered all types of financial data.

Keep track of what types of mail come weekly or monthly (for example, bills). That way, it is easier to see what mail may be missing and possibly stolen. Report missing mail right away to postal officials.

Shred anything that contains your name and address, including credit card offers and statements, utility bills, and expired credit cards or driver's licenses. Remember, thieves do not need much personal information to get started in stealing an identity.

In Public

People are vulnerable to identity theft in any public place. First, carry as little personal information as possible. Purses and wallets often hold a variety of credit cards and other information. People should ask themselves if they need all this documentation every time they leave the house. It is necessary to have five or six credit cards at all times? Is a checkbook needed on every trip out of the house? It is best to downsize whenever possible and take along only the most necessary information. This may include a driver's license and just one credit card. Never take a Social Security card out of a house, unless it is needed to apply for a job.

Be aware of surroundings and nearby people. Shoulder surfing is a practice in which criminals look over someone's shoulder at ATM machines, the grocery store, or any place where someone needs to punch in passwords or PINs. With today's technology, people do not even need to be nearby when shoulder surfing. A digital camera or other recording device can be used from many feet away. Be aware of any suspicious people.

Be careful what information is shared in a cell phone conversation. Some people today have very private conversations even in very public places. People sometimes speak in louder voices on cell phones. If the conversation is private, it is best to talk quietly in a private place to thwart a potential identity thief from eavesdropping.

Keep Track of Important Information

Receipts from credit or debit card transactions are sometimes stuffed into a purse or wallet, or haphazardly tossed into the nearest trash bin. It is important to keep these receipts and check them against statements. A person who faithfully keeps track of all transactions is a person who is more likely to catch identity theft shortly after it happens, thereby minimizing the potential for the crime to spiral out of control.

Staying Safe Online and on the Phone

Never provide unsolicited financial information. In other words, if someone calls and asks for that information, do not give it out. Generally, it is okay to reveal such information if you have initiated the call.

A good option for online purchases is to use a prepaid debit card instead of a credit card. For each purchase made with a debit card, the amount is subtracted from a set amount. This is in contrast to a credit card, in which transactions are added to an account, sometimes up to thousands of dollars. The advantage of using a prepaid debit card is that if the number were stolen, a thief could make purchases only up to the amount on the card. With these prepaid cards, it is a good idea to keep the maximum limit low.

Another tool that can reduce risk of identity theft is eWallet software. This software can be loaded onto a computer or handheld device. It uses encryption technology to store passwords and account numbers. This prevents the need to memorize or write down passwords. It also makes it easy to manage a number of different passwords, helping people avoid the temptation to use the same password for multiple accounts.

If purchases must be made with a credit card, use only one credit card for all online transactions. This will make the transactions easier to track, and consumers can note suspicious activity right away. Many people also choose to use a site such as PayPal to make online purchases. PayPal has millions of customers, and it benefits the company to keep financial data secure. Still, breaches can occur anywhere. People concerned about their information being online might feel safer using a debit card or eWallet software.

Computers should be set to run automatic updates, and the latest version of a browser should always be installed. This will ensure that encryption is up-to-date. Updates that provide additional security patches and other measures are routinely made available. Make sure that any e-retail site uses encryption technology. The business will usually note the use of such technology somewhere on the site. If the site uses encryption, there should be a small lock icon on the bottom navigation bar. Most merchants send consumers an email confirming a purchase. Double-check the email to make sure that everything is correct, and save the email for your records.

Identity Theft Protection Services

The rise in identity theft crime reports has led to a fast-growing business sector: companies that offer identity theft protection services. While some products are legitimate and do help to reduce the risk of identity theft, as with any product, individuals must watch for scams and misleading or false claims.

Advertising tactics by these companies are often aggressive and thereby generate criticism and controversy. For example, one company claims that if individuals use its protection service and still fall prey to identity theft, the company will cover expenses up to $1 million. But in reality, those expenses are related only to settling identity theft matters, not to any losses incurred in the theft itself. One catchy jingle offering free credit reports does not reveal the fact that people have to pay for a service before the free report is delivered to them. Many people have complained to the Federal Trade Commission about signing up for what they thought were free credit reports, only to learn they had been charged.

What these companies generally do not advertise is that they provide services that consumers could do themselves for free. For example, consumers have the legal right to obtain one free credit report each year from all three credit reporting agencies. Consumers can also place fraud alerts and freezes upon their credit reports, again absolutely free. However, keeping on top of one's credit takes time and energy. Some individuals would rather pay companies a fee in exchange for not having to do the work themselves, just as many people pay for the convenience of having someone else change the oil in their cars. Others are willing to pay for the peace of mind of knowing that someone is always monitoring their credit. Consumers who choose this route should carefully research each company and devise a list of questions to ask before signing up for any service.

The following is a list of some identity theft protection services and tips on how to evaluate those services.

Credit Monitoring Services

Under the Fair and Accurate Credit Transactions Act of 2003 (FACTA), consumers can access one free credit report each year from each of the three credit bureaus. But an identity thief can do a lot of damage in a year, so some people choose to get more updates. The three credit reporting agencies also offer more frequent monitoring for $13 to $15 per month. Alternatively, people can hire a company to monitor their reports. The fees and what these businesses provide vary widely. For example, many companies will monitor only one of the credit bureaus, not all three. The Federal Trade Commission recommends carefully reading through a service plan before enrolling. In addition, it is smart to check with a state's attorney general's office or Better Business Bureau to see if there are any complaints on file about the company.

Credit monitoring does not prevent identity theft. It alerts consumers only after identity theft has already occurred, and then only on new accounts. It does not prevent the misuse of existing accounts.

In the past few years, the number of advertisements for "free credit reports" has increased, with entertaining commercials featuring catchy tunes. But the government cautions that there is only one website to trust for the truly free credit report: www.annualcreditreport.com (phone: 1-877-322-8228).

Identity Theft Insurance

These days, more companies are offering identity theft insurance to businesses and individuals. For individuals, a policy typically costs just a few dollars per month. The insurance does not help a consumer avoid identity theft; instead, it covers the costs associated with straightening out an identity theft case. These costs can include telephone calls, copying expenses, mailing expenses, and sometimes legal bills. Insurance companies generally do not reimburse customers for the money that has actually been stolen by an identity thief.

Insurance products purchased through reputable companies are generally reliable, but people should consider the cost of the policy and the deductible (the amount of money a policyholder must pay before the insurance payments begin). For most people, the average cost associated with dealing with identity theft is about $1,500. The amount they pay for the insurance after a couple of years might eclipse any expenses they may occur through identity theft.

In addition, some banks, credit card companies, and homeowner's insurance policies already offer identity theft protection free of charge. Included in this protection are toll-free numbers to call in case of identity theft. Support is also available to help customers close accounts and file fraud reports in the case of stolen identities. While these free protection services may not dole out any financial help, they can offset the need for a lawyer.

Preventing Identity Theft

Fraud Alerts

Under FACTA, anyone can place a fraud alert on his or her credit report, but it lasts just ninety days (unless one can prove himself or herself a victim of identity theft; then the alert lasts for seven years). A number of companies will, for a fee, extend the fraud alert past ninety days.

Fraud alerts require companies to contact an individual before issuing any new lines of credit. This prevents someone from opening new accounts without the rightful owner's knowledge. All credit approvals must come through the account holder.

Victim Assistance

Identity theft victims can take care of resolving the crime on their own, but it takes time, effort, and money. Many reliable resources and centers (including the government's Federal Trade Commission) will assist victims for no charge. Other companies offer this service, but their skills and knowledge vary widely. Victims are urged to fully research these companies and investigate their claims.

Questions to Consider Before Paying for a Service

- Does the company have a good reputation?
- Can you speak to other customers?
- Is there a refund policy?
- What exactly does the service provide (and not provide)?
- Does the company offer a trial period?
- Are there any long-term contracts, or can a consumer cancel at any time?
- What types of complaints, if any, has the company received?

Businesses

Businesses, financial institutions, and organizations are becoming more committed to preventing identity theft in the wake of rising concerns. A recent study showed that the vast majority of people are concerned that a business will sell their personal information. A large number of people, 83 percent, said they worried that information kept by a business will eventually end up in someone else's possession. Another study reported that 69 percent of people would stop doing business with a company that lost their personal data. Consumers want to know that their information will be protected and, given the choice, will patronize businesses that make an effort to secure information.

For example, businesses that use the Merchant Protection Program will display a sign in their windows and cash registers. The program is a service that provides employee training, network scanning for potential risks, and updated policy recommendations.

Businesses such as restaurants are changing the way they process credit card information. Some processing can be done right at the table, so the card never has to leave the cardholder's sight. Other businesses that keep personal financial information in databases are taking measures to encrypt the information or otherwise make it more secure.

Banks can sign up for services that extend identity theft protection to customers. This protection can include giving people access to fraud specialists, assistance with filing claims and placing fraud alerts on accounts and credit reports, and access to educational material including daily threat alerts and monthly newsletters. Generally these services do not charge consumers; the banks pay for the services.

Secure Payment Agent

What if there were a way to make online transactions or conduct banking online without giving out email, password, or account information? This could be done through a secure payment agent. This is a very new field, but it is looking to become a promising, viable means of securing information.

A secure payment agent replaces personal information with anonymous data that disappears after the transaction is complete.

Relying Less on Social Security Numbers

Fewer businesses and agencies are using Social Security numbers to verify identities. Instead, they may assign a different set of numbers to identify individuals. Colleges, which for years used Social Security numbers on posted test score reports and identification cards, are now assigning each student a unique PIN that is not a Social Security number.

Social Security numbers are used in just one of two official ways. For one, employers use them to report data to the Social Security Administration. The agency needs to record the number of hours and years individuals work in order to calculate Social Security benefits upon retirement. In addition, Social Security numbers are used for tax-reporting purposes. Only employers, banking institutions, and select government agencies actually have a legitimate need for Social Security numbers.

Credit Cards

Credit cards are becoming more secure against identity fraud. In addition to the sixteen-digit number on the front of a credit card, there is another, shorter number on the back. Both numbers are usually required before a transaction can be processed. If a thief has only the sixteen-digit number, he or she can do little with it. Of course, crimes can be easily committed if a thief has both numbers or is holding the actual card.

Credit card companies realize the risk of identity theft and the concern it poses for consumers. That is why several companies offer some type of identity theft protection, either free or for a small fee, on accounts. Most credit card companies will assist people in filing reports, identify other attacked accounts, and monitor the case until it is closed. Some credit card companies routinely monitor accounts for suspicious activity and notify cardholders if fraud is suspected. For additional fees, cardholders can get a higher level of protection that might include a daily monitoring of credit reports, notification if fraud is suspected, and identity theft insurance.

Government Laws and Regulations

Some laws relating to identity theft have been in place for years, while other laws are more recent. The high number of identity theft reports in recent years has resulted in federal and state governments taking action against the crimes. But the laws raise a host of interesting questions. How far should the government go in protecting people against identity theft? Does the law go far enough to keep information from falling into the wrong hands? Are the laws even effective? Can the average person understand the complex language in which they are written?

Fair Credit Reporting Act

The Fair Credit Reporting Act (FCRA) was passed in 1970 in response to the fact that credit reporting agencies were slow to act on consumer complaints. Under this law, credit reporting agencies must investigate information that is disputed by a consumer. Information that has been deleted from an account cannot be reinserted without the consumer's knowledge. Negative information about a consumer, such as bankruptcy and tax liens, are not allowed to remain on a report indefinitely. Generally they are removed within seven to ten years.

In addition, this law requires actions on the part of companies and governmental agencies that report information to credit reporting agencies. First, the information must be accurate and complete. Second, if consumers dispute information, the companies must investigate the dispute. Third, companies must notify consumers of negative information within thirty days.

The FCRA also requires that credit reporting agencies give individuals copies of their own credit reports. But the law's scope is surprisingly broad as to who else can obtain credit history information. For example, prospective employers can request credit reports for job applicants. The idea behind this is that employers want to know whether a potential employee is responsible with money or can make good decisions about finances. A poor credit report may indicate otherwise. However, identity theft can affect a credit report through no fault of the individual. Employer access to a poor credit report could cost an applicant the chance of employment. Some states, concerned that this may be an invasion of privacy, are considering legislation that would limit an employer's access to credit reports. Hawaii is one state that has passed this type of legislation.

While bankruptcies more than ten years old and arrests more than seven years old generally do not appear on credit reports, the files still exist. And FCRA is broad enough that some employers can request even that old information if a job pays more than $20,000.

Individuals can either contact the three credit reporting agencies to obtain the reports, or visit the only website that provides credit reports absolutely free: www.annualcreditreport.com.

Electronic Fund Transfer Act

This act, passed in 1978, offers consumers some protection in the case of stolen debit card information. If a victim notifies his or her financial institution of a theft within two business days, he or she is responsible for only $50, no matter how much money was fraudulently withdrawn from the account. However, a victim who waits more than two business days to report a theft may be responsible for up to $500. After sixty days, the victim could be held responsible for all the money that was stolen. It is important to keep a close tab on accounts that are tied to a debit card.

Identity Theft and Assumption Deterrence Act

Congress passed the Identity Theft and Assumption Deterrence Act in 1998. This act contains two important provisions. First, it strengthened laws regarding identity theft criminal cases by allowing the Secret Service, the Federal Bureau of Investigation, and other agencies to prosecute identity theft crimes. In addition, it required the Federal Trade Commission to log consumer complaints, provide victims with informational materials, and refer complaints to the proper agencies (such as consumer reporting agencies and law enforcement officials). Based on this law, the FTC created a toll-free hotline for consumers who suspected identity theft, established a complaint database, and committed itself to educating consumers through booklets and media interviews.

This law was the first to establish that people whose identities are stolen indeed are crime victims. It was also the first law to make identity theft a crime. Generally, under this law, if someone is convicted of using identity theft to aid in any unlawful activity, the sentence is fifteen years in prison and a fine.

Graham-Leach-Bliley Act

The Graham-Leach-Bliley Act of 1999 (also known as the Financial Services Modernization Act) was the first to require financial institutions to keep consumer information private. Each institution must develop privacy policies and inform consumers of those policies at least once a year. Those policies may include a more careful background check of employees with regular access to financial records, or the safeguarding of sensitive documents under lock and key.

Before giving out personal financial information, the financial institution must let the consumer know and give the consumer the choice to "opt out" of such disclosures.

Before this act took place, financial institutions routinely shared consumers' private information not only with affiliated businesses but also with people such as telemarketers. However, the law does not prevent financial institutions from sharing information with affiliated companies. For example, if a bank is affiliated with an insurance company, that insurance company can obtain information from the bank.

One complaint about the Graham-Leach-Bliley Act is that financial institutions must mail disclosures and opt out information, but that customers often cannot decipher the complex language in which such notices are usually written. One survey found that 41 percent of customers did not recall receiving a privacy notice (even though they indeed had received one). Another 22 percent remembered receiving a notice but did not read it. Only .5 percent of customers decided to opt out of the sharing of their personal data. However, proponents of the Graham-Leach-Bliley Act say that the law forces financial institutions to examine their privacy policies, which can result in better changes for consumers.

Customers who want to opt out of sharing personal information can find various form letters on the Internet, which they can tailor and send to their banks or credit card companies. They generally start with, "Please be advised that, in accordance with the Financial Services Modernization Act (Graham-Leach-Bliley Act) you are hereby notified that you do not have my permission to share my personal information with non-affiliated third-party companies or individuals."

The USA PATRIOT Act

The USA PATRIOT Act was passed in 2001 in response to the September 11 terrorist attacks of that year. The USA PATRIOT Act is aimed at giving the government latitude when investigating suspected or known terrorists or terrorist groups. The government implemented these rules because potential terrorists can use alternative identities to forge travel documents and open bank accounts to access large sums of money without suspicion. A portion of the USA PATRIOT Act requires financial institutions to verify the identities of people opening new accounts. In 2003 USA PATRIOT Act rules were finalized to require financial institutions to do three things: One, verify the identity of people opening new accounts; two, keep records of account holders so identities can be verified regularly and quickly; and three, cross-reference account holders with government-provided lists of known or suspected terrorists or terrorist groups.

As with many provisions of the USA PATRIOT Act, these items addressing identity theft cause controversy. Broadly, civil libertarians worry that the USA PATRIOT Act gives government agencies too much latitude when it comes to investigating people they consider "suspicious." How does one define "suspicious behavior"?

Regarding financial records, Federal Bureau of Investigation agents can request such documents through a court order for any investigation into suspected terrorist or intelligence-gathering activities. Under this law, when federal agents request documents from financial institutions, those working at the financial institutions are under a "gag order" to not tell anyone that the documents were requested—not even the account holder. The secret nature of these searches generally arouses the most controversy.

But sometimes agents do not even need a court order to obtain financial records. If an agent deems the records important to national security, he or she simply has to make a written request. These letters are called National Security Letters (NSLs). Anyone who releases these documents to federal agents are under gag orders as well.

FACTA (or FACT Act)

For many years, it was difficult for victims and law enforcement officials to obtain documents (such as account statements showing fraudulent charges) that showed proof of identity theft crimes. Often, police officers had to go through the cumbersome process of obtaining search warrants through court orders to obtain the information. But the Fair and Accurate Credit Transactions Act (FACTA), passed by large majorities in the House and Senate in December 2003 and put into effect a year later, helps identity theft victims on many levels.

FACTA was passed because key provisions of the Fair Credit Reporting Act were set to expire. Legislators feared that if this were allowed to happen, states would start passing their own laws regarding consumer rights and privacy, and those laws might conflict with one another.

FACTA states that victims as well as law enforcement officials have a right to obtain financial documents within thirty days of the receipt of their request. FACTA makes it possible for victims to obtain information related to the theft of their identity without relying on police departments to get those important documents.

The act protects victims by making it easier to report identity theft and set up alerts. For example, a victim needs to make just one call to set up a national fraud alert on his or her credit reports. Based on this call, creditors must contact the victim before setting up new accounts or making changes to existing accounts. And as soon as one credit bureau confirms the fraud, a notice is automatically sent to the other two credit bureaus. The victim will then receive, for free, a credit report from each agency.

The act makes it easier for victims to get information pertaining to the fraudulent transactions. The free credit report allows people to easily obtain their records and keep a closer watch on their accounts. If a victim files a police report, the fraudulent information can be blocked from credit reports.

Under the law, debt collectors have to report fraudulent information to creditors, and creditors and lenders must take action if they receive a report of fraud even if the victim does not recognize it yet.

Since 2007 FACTA has changed the way credit card numbers are printed on receipts. Prior to the law, entire sixteen-digit credit card numbers were printed on receipts for merchandise and other items. But now, only up to the last five digits are permitted to appear, making it more difficult for thieves to obtain account information from receipts. And credit reports may not show more than the last four digits of a Social Security number.

It is argued that consumers are limited when it comes to noticing identity theft. Sometimes businesses are in a better position to flag identity theft before a consumer even suspects it is happening. As a result, in May 2009 new guidelines called "red flag rules" were added to FACTA. These rules require banks to carefully watch accounts for address changes on existing customer accounts, or to take notice when an address provided on a new account differs from the address provided by a credit bureau. Businesses and organizations must have a written plan stating how they will combat and flag identity theft cases. The idea behind the rules is to report suspicious activity before it becomes a full-blown, and costly, case of identity theft. Businesses are already required to protect personal information, but these rules add another layer in trying to prevent identity theft. Financial institutions, such as banks, and creditors (anyone who offers services first and sends a bill later) are expected to follow the red flag rules.

These types of businesses are required to follow four steps when following the new rules:

1. Identify the types of identity theft red flags the business is likely to come across.
2. Set up procedures that will help find suspicious activity on a day-to-day basis.
3. Take appropriate action if red flags are discovered.
4. Keep a written record of the program, and update it frequently.

Breach Laws

Data breaches occur when large numbers of personal records are exposed publicly or fall into the wrong hands. Just because information has been breached does not automatically mean that it will be used to perpetrate identity theft, but it certainly opens the door and makes identity theft more likely to happen.

In 2008 the Identity Theft Resource Center recorded 656 data breaches, which exposed an incredible 35.7 million individual records to the possibility of identity theft. The number of data breaches recorded in 2008 increased 47 percent over the number of reported breaches in 2007.

Many states have passed breach laws that address this growing problem. Breach laws require companies, financial institutions, organizations, and governmental agencies to report data breaches to affected consumers. In July 2003 California was the first state to pass a breach law. As of June 2009 nearly all states—forty-four out of fifty, in addition to the District of Columbia, Puerto Rico, and the Virgin Islands—had enacted breach laws.

In the event of a breach, consumers are usually told that it is a good idea to close the account and open up a new account with new account numbers.

Freeze Laws

A freeze law enables victims to put a freeze on their credit reports. This means that no new lines of credit can be opened because an individual's credit report is "frozen," or unavailable for viewing. Very few creditors will issue new accounts without first being able to check a credit report. A freeze offers people a sense of security if there is ever a time when personal information seems particularly vulnerable (that is, when a person knows that someone is using his/her information, or if personal information has been breached). However, a freeze also means that the individual cannot obtain new credit. If an individual knows that he or she will be applying for credit, a mortgage, a car loan, or the like, a freeze may not be the best option at the time. It is possible to "thaw" a frozen report for a period of time, but the process can take a few days.

As of April 2009, forty-seven states and the District of Columbia have passed freeze laws. Freeze laws vary from state to state, so it is important to check each state's law. Some states allow only identity theft victims to place freezes on credit reports, while other states let all consumers place freezes. Some states require consumers to pay a fee, while in other states the freeze is free.

Encryption Laws

Some states are starting to enact encryption laws. These laws go one step beyond the breach laws, which simply require businesses to notify customers of data breaches. Encryption laws actually require businesses that retain personal and financial information to use software or other devices that protects the information. Encryption makes the data useless and unreadable without a password or another way to access the information. Nevada and Massachusetts are among the first states to adopt such laws. In these states, any business, no matter how big or small, must encrypt personal information and credit card data for transactions that are done electronically.

These state-specific laws affect any business that has customers in those states. For example, if a company based in Indiana has information about a Massachusetts resident, that information needs to be encrypted even though the company itself is not in Massachusetts. Identity theft protection advocates praise these new laws, while some businesses—especially small businesses—worry about the expense involved when investing in encryption software. A laptop computer with an encryption-capable hard drive sells for about $100 more than a regular laptop. Encryption software costs about $50 per computer. Smaller businesses may have to spend a few thousand dollars up front to comply, while larger businesses with many employees and computers may have to invest tens of thousands of dollars.

6 High-Tech Prevention

IRONICALLY, TO PROTECT OUR PERSONAL INFORMAtion, sometimes we have to be willing to give more information. This is the idea that lies behind high-tech identity theft prevention methods. Researchers develop and refine new technologies every day. Those technologies can help law enforcement officials stay one step ahead of identity thieves. But the prevalence of so much information makes some people uncomfortable. In so many aspects of our lives, information about us is compiled digitally—encrypted into magnetic strips on the back of driver's licenses, in computer databases, and stored on Internet servers. Few of us stop to think how much of our information is out there. Some people would argue that there should be less information about us available, while others think that more information will help verify our identities and protect us from thieves. After all, a thief cannot mimic someone's fingerprint or tone of voice. We are not in control of this information. It is compiled by others—government agencies or financial institutions—about us. Should someone other than us have control of our information? What are the dangers? Or is it a way to safeguard our identities?

Biometrics is a relatively new field in which physical characteristics are used to verify identities. These physical characteristics are converted into data and stored in a database. Using physical characteristics allow thieves yet another way in which to access identities. No longer are just Social Security numbers and account numbers vulnerable—with biometrics, our physical information is vulnerable to attack as well. Widespread use of biometrics would someday reduce the need for people to carry around credit cards or enter account information online to make purchases. Biometrics would eliminate the use of identifying numbers in general, whether they are Social Security numbers, PINs, or military identification numbers.

Some people contend that biometric technology is a safe, nearly foolproof way to verify identities. Research shows that most people favor biometrics as a way to safeguard against identity theft. The technology services company Unisys released survey results in 2008 showing that 70 percent of people would not mind if a bank or government agency used biometrics to verify identification. When it comes to preferred identification, fingerprints rank nearly as high as passwords.

On the other hand, privacy advocates worry that this information can fall into the wrong hands. Will identification through physical characteristics result in bias according to race or gender? What is to stop law enforcement agencies from secretly using the information in crime investigations? Members of the public are rightly concerned about how much private information should be gathered and how it will be treated.

It is important first to understand the different aspects of biometrics and how physical information can be used in different ways to verify identity.

Fingerprinting

Fingerprinting has been in use for many decades, most often to identify and catch criminals. But now officials are looking toward fingerprinting as a way to safeguard identities. For example, a motor vehicles department could retain a database of fingerprints and ask people to scan their fingerprints when applying for a driver's license.

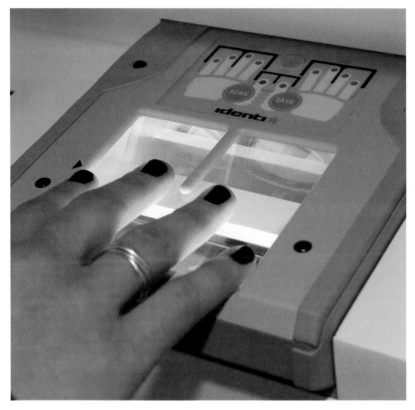

This fingerprint-scanning machine is used at airport security checkpoints.

Companies and government agencies are using fingerprint technology to verify employee identities and to perform background checks. For example, before hiring teachers and other staff members, school districts often require background checks be done by the use of fingerprinting. Prospective employees have to agree to the checks. If they refuse, they cannot be hired. Because so much identity theft occurs in the workplace, having a more secure background check through fingerprints can screen out job candidates with questionable backgrounds. Using fingerprint identity checks within the workplace can also make high-security facilities more secure and lessen the threat that unauthorized users will gain access to secure computers or areas.

Fingerprints can also enable customers to pay by touch instead of carrying cash or credit cards. In this method, the fingerprint is linked to account information, so the bill's total is automatically withdrawn from the account. This payment option has been slow to catch on, however, because of privacy concerns and expense. For a while, some stores across the nation—select Cub Foods stores and Jewel-Osco stores—were using pay-by-touch technology. However, the company offering the technology went out of business in 2008.

The main argument against using fingerprints to verify identity is the concern that fingerprints will be used in other ways. Privacy advocates want to know that fingerprint information will not be shared in violation of individuals' constitutional right to privacy. For example, what if the Federal Bureau of Investigation seeks fingerprint records to pursue criminal probes, or if the Immigration and Naturalization Service wants the data to verify citizenship status?

Retinal Scans and Iris Recognition

It may sound like something from a futuristic movie, but technology can be used to scan eyes to provide another layer of identity theft protection. Parts of the eyes scanned include the retina and the iris.

A retinal scan uses technology to look at a person's eyeball, quickly measuring patterns of blood vessels that are unique to each individual. Retinal scans are generally reliable, as eyes do not change (though problems such as glaucoma and cataracts can interfere with readings). A retinal scan, however, is expensive and time-consuming. A person being scanned must sit still for several moments while an infrared beam scans the eye. In the future, computers may be outfitted with retinal scan capabilities to verify identities for people shopping or banking online.

Iris recognition technology is a bit simpler than retinal scan technology. In an iris scan, a video camera takes a picture of a person's iris. An iris—the colored part of the eye—is unique to each

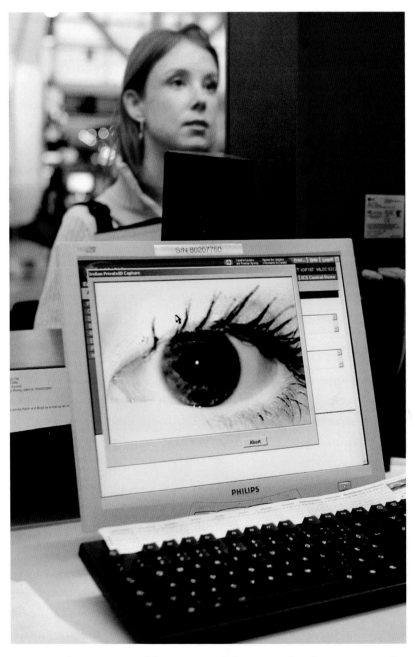

A reporter has a picture of her iris recorded as part of a demonstration of iris recognition biometric technology being used at the Vancouver (British Columbia, Canada) International Airport.

individual. However, if a pupil is dilated or if a person is wearing colored contact lenses, the information is less reliable.

Many companies have begun to offer iris recognition software to financial institutions as a way to fight identity theft. Cairo Amman Bank in Jordan was the first to enable customers to use iris scans as a way to verify identity to withdraw money from accounts instead of swiping a card.

Voice Verification

Voice recognition allows people to identify themselves through their voice. However, this technology has a few drawbacks. Voices change over time, much more than a fingerprint or an eye scan does. While it can be difficult, there is also the possibility that voices can be imitated. Or a recording of someone's voice can be used to try to beat the system.

DNA Testing

Another controversial method of identity verification is the use of DNA testing. DNA is obtained physically through a blood sample, a cheek swab, or a strand of hair. DNA testing can be used to confirm data on birth certificates, verifying the identity of a person's parents.

It was recently discovered that Major League Baseball officials use DNA testing to verify the identities and ages of foreign baseball prospects. In the past, players from outside the United States have used forged birth certificates to claim they are younger than they really are. A sixteen-year-old player looks more promising to officials—and can may be offered a more lucrative, longer contract—than a nineteen-year-old or twenty-year-old player, for example. To get around these forgeries, baseball prospects from foreign countries are subjected to DNA tests that confirm their parentage to verify their birth certificate information. In some cases, these players are also subjected to bone scans that can be used to verify age.

Opponents of such tests worry that they will be used to determine future medical conditions. For example, DNA information can reveal a susceptibility to cancer or injury—information that team officials might take into consideration when offering a contract.

Federal legislation set to take effect in November 2009 would prohibit DNA tests on the part of U.S. employers. However, it is not clear whether employers, such as Major League Baseball, could conduct the tests on foreign prospects.

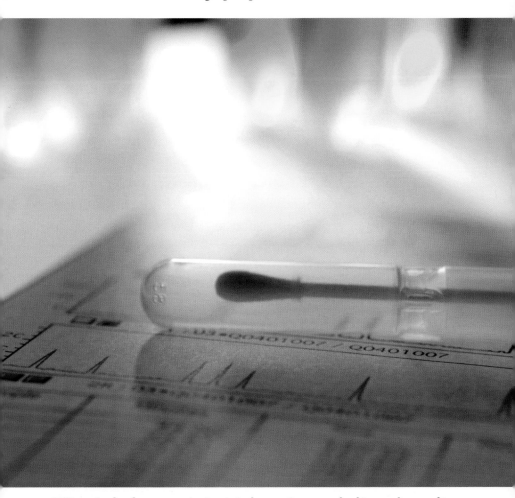

DNA testing has become routine in criminal cases. Some people object to the use of it for identity recognition, seeing it as a violation of civil and privacy rights.

National Biometric Security Project

The National Biometric Security Project (NBSP) was established after the terrorist attacks of September 11, 2001. The attacks raised concerns that countries were vulnerable to attacks perpetrated by people who have stolen identities to cross borders and finance their terrorist networks. NBSP aims to help businesses and government agencies employ biometric technology as a tool for identity verification. The nonprofit organization tests biometric products to ensure that they meet requirements. It also provides training services to people interested in using biometric technology in their business or organization. In Morgantown, West Virginia, the NBSP operates Biometric Services International. This laboratory develops and tests biometric technology and provides support for further research in the field. The lab is the only one like it in the United States.

Other Technology

Any unique characteristic is fodder for recognition technology. Some of the more recent advances including scanning the veins in a person's hand, or using devices that measure the individual geometric shape of a hand. Other devices measure different points on an ear to come up with a unique result for each individual.

But these high-tech options for fighting identity theft do not come without some concerns. For one, no database is safe from hackers and thieves. An enterprising criminal can find a way to access biometric databases, just as criminals have been able to access systems that store thousands of credit card numbers. It is difficult to come up with a foolproof, theft-resistant database.

Biometric information might not always work. There are cases where the biometric scan and information in the database do not match, even when they both belong to the same person. Imagine the frustration in trying to access a bank account but being denied because of a computer error.

Still, there is no doubt that biometrics is a growing trend. We likely will see identity verification through biometrics continue to gain popularity. Already, a few universities around the country offer degrees in biometrics. This major combines biology and computer courses to give students information they need to find jobs in this emerging field.

National Identity Card

Every so often, debate arises in the United States about the need for a national identity card. A national identity card would use fingerprints or other biometric information to verify the identity of the cardholder. While the idea has taken off in Europe, debate has stalled in the United States because of privacy concerns. Surveys reveal that the American public is split on this issue. The Pew Research Center found that in 2006, 56 percent of Americans favored the issuance of national identity cards.

Driver's licenses are often used to verify identity, but not everyone has a driver's license. Social Security numbers, too, are used to identify people, but more governmental agencies and businesses are relying less on the numbers. These documents are also easily forged. Terrorists who want to gain access to secure areas can obtain multiple forged driver's licenses by faking birth certificates. By tying biometric information to an identity card, the risk of forgery goes down.

In the days after the September 11 terrorist attacks in the United States, leading politicians and bureaucrats said that if everyone presented a national identity card before boarding a plane, risks of future attacks would be lessened. Advocates said the trade-off for less privacy was increased security. Some continue to believe that, while others insist that the privacy of all citizens should be top priority. Finding the right balance between privacy and security is an ongoing quest.

7 Identity Theft Around the World

THE UNITED STATES IS HARDLY ALONE IN REPORTS OF identity theft. Personal information of anyone, anywhere, can be stolen at a moment's notice. The Internet, especially, is collapsing geographic boundaries. Identity thieves can work from anywhere and obtain information about a person who is living down the street or halfway around the globe.

Identity theft crimes can quickly breed in developing countries. There, government officials do not have the means or capabilities to investigate online fraud. This allows enterprising criminals to set up shop with little interference or oversight. Countries that are often host to identity theft rings include Ukraine, Indonesia, Yugoslavia, and Lithuania. Many countries have lax security or little oversight when it comes to Internet security.

Consumers in some countries appear to be more vulnerable to identity theft than those in other countries. A recent report showed that online consumers in Canada, the United States, and the United Kingdom were more vulnerable to identity theft than people in France, Spain, or Germany. The survey revealed perhaps one explanation: consumers in Canada, the United States and the United Kingdom, for some reason, are more likely to share passwords than consumers in other countries.

Though hard data is not available, anecdotal evidence has led experts to believe that identity theft occurs less in Europe than in the United States. Officials in the United States could take some ideas from European countries that might reduce instances of identity theft. The sheer number of businesses in the United States, governmental bureaucracy, and privacy concerns sometimes limit implementation of identity theft prevention measures.

The following may explain why Europeans at times are less vulnerable to identity theft than residents in the United States:

- Most Europeans are identified by a national identity number. This number is used far less than Social Security numbers in the United States. Europeans know to keep their identification numbers private and use them only when necessary or required by law.

- Credit is more difficult to obtain in Europe. European financial institutions do not have access to quick credit reports that are available in the United States. The process to authorize credit in Europe is much slower and allows time to verify the identity of the person making the request. This may result in less convenience for the consumer, but it also means it is more difficult for someone to open up credit lines under a false name.

- Europeans rely less on credit cards than U.S. citizens. Europeans are more likely to use a debit card that withdraws money from an account, rather than charge money and add it to an account until it reaches a high limit. If an identity thief does obtain a debit card, the damage he or she can incur is usually less than is possible with a stolen credit card number. Europeans also use "smart cards" in which magnetic strips are replaced by small computer chips. This makes them less susceptible to tampering and fraud. Because Europeans use fewer credit cards, they get fewer credit card offers in the mail. This means there is less risk of an identity thief filling out a blank application.

- Less information is shared. In the United States, companies routinely sell database information to other companies. This is one reason people receive a lot of junk mail and telemarketing calls. The more that information floats around for others to see, the more likely it is to be intercepted and used by an identity thief. European laws are stricter and generally do not allow companies to sell or share information.

Laws regarding identity theft differ from country to country. Some countries, such as the United Kingdom, are already using advanced technology to combat identity theft, while others are not. Here is a sample of how some larger, more populated countries around the world deal with identity theft.

Canada

Canada does not have any nationwide laws that criminalize identity theft, despite the fact that a report issued in late 2008 stated that 1.7 million Canadians had been victims of identity theft in the previous year. In early 2009 government officials announced legislation that would make identity theft a crime. Canada does not have any antispam email legislation. Spammers take advantage of this fact, and many spam emails that ask people to reveal personal account information originate in Canada.

United Kingdom

By early 2008 it was estimated that 4 million Britons were victims of identity theft. The United Kingdom's rules regarding identity theft are a little different from those in the United States. In the case of stolen credit card information, the victim first reports the crime to the credit card company. The company is responsible for investigating the crime and clearing the victim's record. The company may elect to report the incident to the local law enforcement agency,

In 2004, Tony Blair, then prime minister of the United Kingdom, held up a biometric identity card. Though making such cards mandatory has been discussed, the program has not been implemented there.

but it is not required to do so. If the crime does not involve credit cards, it still is reported first to whatever relevant organization was involved in the crime, and then to the local police. The burden of investigating the theft is taken off the consumer, unlike in the United States. This leads to a question: Who is better suited to report and investigate identity theft: consumers or financial institutions?

The United Kingdom is one country that has talked about using national identity cards to verify a person's identity. Each card would be linked to a biometric record of a person's face and fingerprints. The program's intent is to reduce the risk of identity theft and eliminate the need for a person to carry around several identifying documents. Sweden and Finland are two other European countries that use smart cards as national identification.

National IDs and smart cards tend to find success in Europe because of the relative ease of instituting them. For example, just five or six banking institutions dominate the European financial market; in contrast, the United States has more than ten thousand banks. So one bank in Europe that wants to implement smart card technology immediately reaches a large segment of the population. Smart cards actually started in Europe with nationally run telephone companies. If people wanted to make a phone call, they had to use a smart card, putting smart cards in the hands of millions of customers all at once.

However, the United Kingdom is not without large identity theft crime rings, which can also be found in the United States and in other parts of the world. For example, in 2005 it was revealed that businessman Anton Gelonkin had used the identities of hundreds of dead children to defraud Britons of millions of dollars for his crime ring.

In 2008 the United Kingdom formed the National Fraud Strategic Authority (NFSA) to combat identity theft. The NFSA is charged with making the country less hospitable to identity theft crimes. The organization looks at ways to fight identity theft and protect the public. Because of the new measures, in one year the Metropolitan Police Service stopped ten separate criminal networks in London that were creating false identity cards. These criminals were charged under the 2006 Identity Cards Acts, which prohibits the use of false identity documents.

Hong Kong

Hong Kong is one of Asia's biggest finance hubs, and as a result it has seen a slight increase in identity theft reports. TransUnion Hong Kong, the country's only credit reporting agency, holds 4 million records. It reported just twenty cases of identity theft in the first three months of 2009. That year, police uncovered a large gang operation that was stealing financial information to commit fraud totaling $80,000 Hong Kong dollars ($10,300 U.S. dollars).

Hong Kong officials urge people to beware of phishing schemes and never to reveal personal financial information over the phone or the Internet.

Since 2003 Hong Kong residents have been able to obtain credit reports, much as U.S. citizens can. Hong Kong officials also urge residents to check credit reports to see if anything is amiss regarding their financial records.

China

Identity theft in China is more likely to revolve around obtaining jobs and education rather than be used to commit financial fraud. China's government system has led to widespread corruption and abuses of power, which can breed identity theft. A recent case serves as a good example.

In 2004 Luo Caixia, a top student, was admitted to Guizhou Normal University. However, Luo never received her admittance letter and believed that she had not been accepted. Unknown to her, a classmate named Wang Jiajun took her place and attended the university under Luo's name. Meanwhile, Luo was accepted by another university. She did not learn of the identity theft until several years later, when she tried to open a bank account and was told her personal information was already in use.

It was discovered that Wang Jiajun's father, Wang Zhengrong, had paid to have the identities of the girls switched so that his daughter—who had poor grades—could go to college. The father was a local police official and was detained on charges of using his power to forge documents. The case has sparked nationwide media attention in China. While similar cases in the past have resulted in just small fines or no punishment at all, Wang Zhengrong's detention is seen as a signal that abuses of authority will no longer be tolerated.

Overall in Asia, security lags behind what is offered in the United States and Western Europe. This allows people to take advantage of the Internet to perpetrate identity theft. For example,

Luo Caixia, a top student in China, was the victim of a particularly nasty identity theft—because the perpetrator of the crime was a police officer!

wireless networks tend to be less secure, which makes them vulnerable to hackers who then obtain personal information that is sent over the networks.

Other countries do not have a clear chain of command when it comes to financial information. In the Philippines, for example, people who have complaints about suspicious ATMs are not sure where to direct their complaints because it is not clear which banks own which machines.

Australia

The Australian government recognizes the damage that identity theft inflicts upon its citizens and is taking new measures to limit instances of identity theft within the country's borders. The Identity Security branch of the Australian Attorney General's office is responsible for implementing strategies that reduce the risk of identity theft.

The government has launched a National Identity Security Strategy, which promotes the idea of a national identity card and biometric security measures. In addition, a document verification service is a secure online database used by governmental agencies to check the accuracy and legitimacy of documents presented as proof of identity. The government has also created an identity theft kit available to all Australians that educates them about identity theft, how to prevent it, and what steps to take if it happens.

Traveling Abroad

Does traveling make a person more vulnerable to identity theft? The simple fact is that identity theft can happen anywhere, at any time. It can happen while people are on vacation, either in their own country or in a foreign country. Foreign travel may pose a higher risk of identity theft because travelers who are unfamiliar with a country and language may become distracted and less aware of their personal possessions.

Travelers should bring only necessary documents. Chances are travelers can leave checks and extra credit cards at home. The Identity Theft Resource Center recommends that travelers do not carry any documents that list their Social Security numbers.

Keep careful watch over laptops, wallets, and purses. In hotel rooms, take advantage of a room safe if there is one, and lock all personal possessions and documents in the safe when you are not in the room. Be aware of and alert to all surroundings. Sometimes tourists are easy to spot, making them likely victims for pickpockets. Know where personal items are at all times and keep them in a secure place on the body when out in public.

Keep photocopies of important documents, such as driver's licenses and passports, and store them in a separate location from the originals. Travel can become difficult and problematic if these identity documents are stolen.

Back at home, make sure mail and newspaper delivery are put on hold or collected by a neighbor. Mail that piles up in mailboxes is an easy target for identity thieves. And a mound of newspapers outside a front door provides a signal to thieves who may break in and steal not only possessions but also identifying documents they find lying around.

Tracking Down International Identity Theft

Officials in the United States have the authority to pursue international criminals when identity theft is perpetrated upon U.S. citizens. U.S. law enforcement officials work with officers of the INTERPOL, which is an international criminal police organization. INTERPOL represents 188 countries.

The biggest bust of an identity theft crime ring to date involved several international suspects. In late 2008 millions of consumers received a letter in the mail. The letter stated that their credit card information had been breached and consumers should take steps to close the potentially vulnerable accounts.

Russian Business Network

One of the largest and most notorious Internet-based identity fraud crime rings is known as the Russian Business Network (RBN).

Authorities have named the network and identified its base as St. Petersburg, Russia, but little else is known about the organization. Those who run it use only nicknames; the mastermind is known as "Flyman." Their Internet domains are registered to anonymous addresses, and their transactions are untraceable.

The RBN sells website hosting for gangs and individuals who use the sites to commit crimes. This criminal activity can take many forms, including identity theft scams. Those operating through RBN-run websites are thought to be responsible for half of all phishing schemes, security experts say. In 2006 users of the network managed to steal $150 million from bank accounts.

The RBN is notorious for sending unsuspecting victims to phishing sites, where it then collects personal information. It even has created "antispyware" software that people download, believing they are protecting themselves from harmful spyware. But RBN's antispyware is actually just another way to gain access to people's personal information.

Experts believe the group may have ties to the Russian criminal underground and corrupt politicians. Countries that have no laws or few laws against identity theft and cybercrime provide an opportunity for identity theft criminals to flourish. In addition, the United States has found that Russian authorities are unwilling to cooperate with investigations of the RBN.

Albert Gonzalez is thought to be the mastermind behind the theft of credit and debit cards from 40 million people. It took the U.S. government three years to solve the case.

Authorities charged eleven people with stealing credit card information from 40 million individuals. The criminals allegedly accessed databases at large retailers such as TJ Maxx, Office Max, and Barnes and Noble. U.S. Department of Justice officials estimated that tens of millions of dollars may have been stolen using people's credit cards.

Because it was such a large crime ring, it took investigators more than three years to crack the case. The eleven people charged lived all over the world—China, Ukraine, Turkey, and Germany. The ringleader is thought to be a man named Albert Gonzalez, who lived in Miami at the time of the bust.

Notes

Introduction

p. 6, "The U.S. Department of Justice . . .": Identity Theft Resource Center, "Workplace Facts and Statistics," 2009, www.idtheftcenter. org/workplace_facts.html (accessed March 26, 2009).

p. 6, "The Federal Trade Commission (FTC) estimates . . .": Federal Trade Commission, "About Identity Theft," www.ftc.gov/bcp/edu/microsites/idtheft/consumers/about-identity theft.html (accessed December 28, 2008).

Chapter 1

p. 10, "Some have even been arrested . . .": Synovate, "Federal Trade Commission 2006 Identity Theft Survey Report," November 2007, www.ftc.gov/os/2007/11/SynovateFinalReportIDTheft2006.pdf (accessed January 2, 2009).

p. 10, "Before committing suicide . . .": "Shipping Board Embezzler, Killing Himself, Wrote That He Assumed a Dead Man's Name," *New York Times*, November 25, 1923.

p. 11, "In 2008 the highest percentage. . .": *Consumer Sentinel Network Data Book for January–December 2008*, Federal Trade Commission, February 2009, 14.

p. 11, "But those nineteen and under . . .": *Consumer Sentinel Network Data Book for January–December 2008*, Federal Trade Commission, 14.

p. 12, "The Federal Trade Commission reports . . .": Joe Light, "Children Targeted in Surging Numbers," *Boston Globe*, July 10, 2005.

p. 12, "Friesen now travels the country . . .": Brian Dakss, "Kids' ID Theft: A Growing Problem," CBS News Early Show, January 16, 2006, www.cbsnews.com/stories/2006/01/15/earlyshow/living/ConsumerWatch/main1210020.shtml (accessed August 5, 2009).

p. 13, "The National Center on Elder Abuse . . .": The National Center on Elder Abuse, "The 2004 Survey of State Adult Protective Services: Abuse of Adults 60 Years of Age and Older," February 2006, www.ncea.aoa.gov/NCEAroot/Main_Site/pdf/2-14-06%20FINAL%2060+REPORT.pdf (accessed August 5, 2009).

p. 13, "Another target for identity thieves . . .": "Protecting Deceased or Ill Loved Ones from Identity Theft," *Business Wire*, January 26, 2009.

p. 14, "One out of five identity theft scams . . .": Eileen Ambrose, "College Students Should Study Up on ID Theft: 1 Out of 5 Data Breaches Occurs in School Setting," *Chicago Tribune*, September 7, 2008.

p. 14, "A UCLA official said . . .": Rebecca Trounson, "FBI Site to Aid UCLA Hacker Probe," *Los Angeles Times*, December 16, 2006.

p. 14, "In March 2009 Iona College . . .": "Iona College Becomes the First to Create a 'Data Breach-Free Campus' and Provide Proactive Identity Theft Protection to Students, Faculty and Staff," *Business Wire*, March 2, 2009.

p. 16, "Statistics show that 75 percent . . .": Teresa M. McAleavy, "Meeting in Hackensack, N.J., to Focus on Ways to Stop Workplace Identity Theft," *Knight Ridder Tribune Business News*, May 20, 2004.

p. 17, "The Identity Theft Resource Center has estimated . . .": Identity Theft Resource Center, "Workplace Facts and Statistics," 2009, www.idtheftcenter.org/workplace_facts.html (accessed March 26, 2009).

p. 20, "Facebook is undoubtedly . . .": "Pressroom," Facebook,

2009, www.facebook.com/press/info.php?statistics (accessed April 28, 2009).

p. 21, "Some sites are set up to mimic . . .": Kim Hart, "Phish-Hooked; Thieves Find Easy Pickings on Social Sites," *Washington Post*, July 16, 2006.

p. 21, "Thieves can portray themselves . . .": Hart, "Phish-Hooked," July 16, 2006.

p. 21, "Or when scammers get people to . . .": , Hart, "Phish-Hooked," July 16, 2006.

p. 22, "According to the Federal Trade Commission, Arizona . . .": *Consumer Sentinel Network Data Book for January–December 2008*, Federal Trade Commission, February 2009, 14.

p. 22, "The top three U.S. metropolitan areas . . .": *Consumer Sentinel Network Data Book for January–December 2008*, Federal Trade Commission, 16.

p. 23, "Places that see a lot of drug activity . . .": Jennifer Mulrean, "DollarWise: The Worst States for Identity Theft," *MSN Money*, http://moneycentral.msn.com/content/Banking/FinancialPrivacy/P125094.asp (accessed April 19, 2009).

p. 24, "Officials from the site . . .": Barbara Ortutay, "Facebook Plans to Simplify Privacy Settings," ABC Local, July 1, 2009, http://abclocal.go.com/ktrk/story?section=news/technology&id=6894261 (accessed January 25, 2010).

p. 24, "Millions of these types of transactions . . .": Bruce Horovitz, "Restaurants Tighten Credit Card Security; Efforts Made to Guard Against Identity Theft," *USA Today*, March 5, 2007.

p. 24, "A thief later downloads . . .": Mark Peters, "Identity Theft's Newest Bite–At Maine Restaurants; Diners at Two Restaurants Report Finding Bogus Charges on Credit-Card Bills. Police Suspect 'Skimmers' Were Used," *Portland Press Herald*, June 26, 2005.

p. 24, "It was discovered that she . . .": Stuart Silverstein, "Ex-Waitress Allegedly Swiped Patrons' Identities; More Than $16,000 in False Charges Were Made Using Numbers Stolen at a West

L.A. Eatery," *Los Angeles Times*, May 22, 2007.

p. 25, "And people who report. . .": Peters, "Identity Theft's Newest Bite," June 26, 2005.

p. 25, "Instead, encrypted data rather than actual . . .": Horovitz, "Restaurants Tighten Credit Card Security," March 5, 2007.

p. 25, "Dozens of restaurant chains . . .": Horovitz, "Restaurants Tighten Credit Card Security," March 5, 2007.

Chapter 2

p. 27, "When thieves use information . . .": Synovate, "Federal Trade Commission 2006 Identity Theft Survey Report," Federal Trade Commission, November 2007, www.ftc.gov/os/2007/11/Synovate-FinalReportIDTheft2006.pdf (accessed January 2, 2009).

p. 28, "A 2007 medical journal . . .": Latour "LT" Lafferty, "Medical Identity Theft: The Future Threat of Health Care Fraud Is Now," *Journal of Health Care Compliance*, 9, 1, 2007, 11.

p. 28, "The number of fraud . . .": Lafferty, "Medical Identity Theft: The Future Threat of Health Care Fraud Is Now," 2007, 12.

p. 28, "Health care records . . .": Lafferty, "Medical Identity Theft: The Future Threat of Health Care Fraud Is Now," 2007, 15.

p. 28, "These people may have . . .": Reba L. Kieke, "Although a Relatively New Risk Area, Medical Identity Theft Should Not Be Taken Lightly," *Journal of Health Care Compliance*, 11, 1, 2009, 51–74.

p. 29, "This careful oversight . . .": Kieke, "Although a Relatively New Risk Area, Medical Identity Theft Should Not Be Taken Lightly," 2009, 51–74.

p. 31, "Purchases included a plasma television . . .": Josh Poltilove and Thomas W. Krause, "Ex-Marine Takes Plea Deal in Thefts," *McClatchy-Tribune Business News*, August 20, 2008.

p. 32, "A system of checks and balances . . .": Kieke, "Although a Relatively New Risk Area, Medical Identity Theft Should Not Be Taken Lightly," 51–74.

p. 32, "They theorize that perhaps . . .": David Klepper, "Identity

Theft Increasingly Linked to Illegal Immigration," *McClatchy-Tribune Business News*, April 23, 2008.

p. 33, "One Social Security number could be used . . .": Christine Tatum and Kieran Nicholson, "Hard Lesson: Carelessness Opens Door to ID Thieves," *Denver Post*, December 13, 2006.

p. 33, "It turns out that her identity . . .": Klepper, "Identity Theft Increasingly Linked to Illegal Immigration," April 23, 2008.

p. 33, "Even if employers doubt . . .": Tatum and Nicholson, "Hard Lesson," December 13, 2006.

p. 33, "Even if officials suspect . . .": Klepper, "Identity Theft Increasingly Linked to Illegal Immigration," April 23, 2008.

p. 34, "Already, the city of . . .": Emily Bazar, "Illegal Immigrants Are Issued ID Cards in Some Places," *USA Today*, October 4, 2007, www.usatoday.com/news/nation/2007-10-03-Immigrant_N.htm (accessed August 8, 2009).

p. 35, "Federal, state, and local agencies . . .": Klepper, "Identity Theft Increasingly Linked to Illegal Immigration," April 23, 2008.

p. 35, "A 2006 Colorado investigation . . .": Tatum and Nicholson, "Hard Lesson," December 13, 2006.

p. 36, "Of that number . . .": Adam Liptak and Julia Preston, "Supreme Court Hears Challenge to Identity theft Law in Immigration Cases," *New York Times*, February 25, 2009, www.nytimes.com/2009/02/26/us/26identity.html?_r=1&scp=1&sq=identity%20theft%20immigration%20supreme%20court&st=cse (accessed May 4, 2009).

p. 36, "In May 2009 . . .": David Stout, "Supreme Court Rules Against Government in Identity theft Case," *New York Times*, May 4, 2009, www.nytimes.com/2009/05/05/us/05scotus.html (accessed May 4, 2009).

p. 38, "And if businesses could find a way . . .": Identity Theft Resource Center, "ITRC 2009 Consumer Awareness Survey: The Need for 'Secure Payment Agent' (SPA)," May 19, 2009, www.

idtheftcenter.org/artman2/publish/lib_survey/SPA_White_Paper. shtml (accessed May 26, 2009).

p. 39, "This mistake affected . . .": Identity Theft Resource Center, " Data Breaches," 2009, www.idtheftcenter.org/artman2/publish/lib_ survey/ITRC_2008_Breach_List.shtml#breaches (accessed April 21, 2009).

p. 39, "False passports and other . . .": "Testimony of Dennis M. Lormel, Chief, Terrorist Financial Review Group, FBI, Before the Senate Judiciary Committee Subcommittee on Technology, Terrorism and Government Information July 9, 2002," *Federal Bureau of Investigation*, July 9, 2002, www.fbi.gov/congress/congress02/ idtheft.htm (accessed March 3, 2009).

Chapter 3

p. 42, "People should be aware . . .": Michael J. Arata Jr., *Preventing 42 Theft for Dummies*, Indianapolis: Wiley Publishing, Inc., 2004, 121–123.

p. 43, "They most often strike . . .": Arata Jr., *Preventing Identity Theft for Dummies*, 172.

p. 43, "The only time people . . .": Arata Jr., *Preventing Identity Theft for Dummies*, 173.

p. 44, "Some experts believe . . .": Bill Myers, "Identity Theft Swells in District, Nation as Economy Plummets," *Washington Examiner*, March 9, 2009, www.washingtonexaminer.com/local/Identitytheft-swells-in-District-nation-as-economy-plummets-40931777.html (accessed August 5, 2009).

p. 44, "Thieves are still charging . . .": Jordan Robertson, "Identity Theft Still Big Business," *South Florida Sun Sentinel*, April 15, 2009.

p. 45, "In addition, U.S. Census workers . . .": Katherine Calos, "Census Workers Mindful of Identity theft Fears," *McClatchy-Tribune Business News*, May 5, 2009.

p. 46, "A legitimate charity . . .": Arata Jr., *Preventing Identity Theft for Dummies*, 175.

p. 47, "These usually do not include . . .": Arata Jr., *Preventing Identity Theft for Dummies*, 176.

p. 47, "A live person . . .": Arata Jr., *Preventing Identity Theft for Dummies*, 176.

p. 47, "A bank would never close . . .": Arata Jr., *Preventing Identity Theft for Dummies*, 177.

p. 49, "Most of those crimes . . .": "Consumer Reports Survey: One in Five Online Consumers Have Been Victims of Cybercrime," *PR Newswire*, May 4, 2009.

p. 49, "The same survey . . .": "Consumer Reports Survey," May 4, 2009.

p. 51, "For example, Verizon allows . . .": "Verizon: Verizon Internet Security Suite Adds Wi-Fi Security, Advance Protection for Broadband Customers; New Capabilities Position Award-Winning Verizon Software as One of Most Comprehensive Internet Security Suites on the Market," *M2 Presswire*, May 1, 2009.

p. 52, "At any one time . . .": Rebecca Sausner, "B of A: Phishing Victims Won't Get Fooled Again," *American Banker*, May 5, 2009.

p. 52, "This page tells customers . . .": Sausner, "B of A," May 5, 2009.

p. 52, "Seven months after . . .": Sausner, "B of A," May 5, 2009.

p. 53, "The operations became more sophisticated . . .": "A Brief History of Phishing," *Washington Post*, November 18, 2004, www.washingtonpost.com/wp-dyn/articles/A59350-2004Nov18.html (accessed August 24, 2009).

p. 53, "For example, violation of . . .": "Governor Signs Anti-Phishing Law," *Knight Ridder Tribune Business News*, August 24, 2007.

p. 54, "Plans are in place . . .": Sausner, "B of A," May 5, 2009.

p. 54, "The number of phishing websites . . .": Anti-Phishing Working Group, "Phishing Activity Trends Report: 2nd Half

2008," www.antiphishing.org/reports/apwg_report_H2_2008.pdf (accessed February 20, 2009).

p. 54, "A *Consumer Reports* survey . . .": "*Consumer Reports* Survey," May 4, 20009.

p. 54, "One such scam . . .": Deborah Buckhalter, "Scammers Now Using Text Msgs," *McClatchy-Tribune Business News*, February 25, 2009.

p. 55, "They try to get tellers . . .": "Social Engineering, Cyber-crime Will Be Challenges in 2009, Predicts Identity Theft Assistance Center," *Business Wire*, December 2, 2008.

Chapter 4

p. 61, "How best to resolve . . .": Identity Theft Resource Center, "Fact Sheet 106: Organizing Your Identity Theft Case," April 28, 2007, www.idtheftcenter.org/artman2/publish/v_fact_sheets/ Fact_Sheet_106_Organizing_Your_Identity_Theft_Case.shtml (accessed January 22, 2009).

p. 61, "According to a Federal Trade Commission survey . . .": Federal Trade Commission, "2006 Identity Theft Survey Report," November 2007, www.ftc.gov/os/2007/11/SynovateFinalReport IDTheft2006.pdf (accessed March 2, 2009).

p. 62, "And if the thief was a relative . . .": Identity Theft Resource Center, "Fact Sheet 108: Overcoming the Emotional Impact," April 28, 2007, www.idtheftcenter.org/artman2/publish/v_fact_sheets/ Fact_Sheet_108_Overcoming_The_Emotional_Impact.shtml (accessed March 22, 2009).

p. 64, "But officials at the . . .": Identity Theft Resource Center, "Fact Sheet 115: When You Personally Know the Identity Thief," May 2, 2007, www.idtheftcenter.org/artman2/publish/v_fact_sheets/ Fact_Sheet_115_When_you_personallyknow_the_identity_thief. shtml (accessed March 22, 2009).

p. 66, "In the 1960s . . .": "About Frank Abagnale," *Abagnale and Associates*, 1999–2009, www.abagnale.com/aboutfrank.htm (accessed March 3, 2009).

p. 66, "Authorities think that Abdallah . . .": "Cybertheft Case Skewers Celebs," CBSNews.com, March 20, 2001, www.cbsnews.com/stories/2001/03/20/archive/technology/main280107.shtml (accessed March 3, 2009).

p. 67, "Then he called the provider . . .": Bob Sullivan, "ID Thief to the Stars Tells All," MSNBC.COM, www.msnbc.msn.com/id/5763781 (accessed March 3, 2009).

p. 67, "Jackson, like Abagnale . . .": Allan Koay, "From Convict to Crusader," *The Star Online*, Maylasia, September 29, 2008, http://thestar.com.my/lifestyle/story.asp?file=/2008/9/29/lifefocus/1908008&sec=lifefocus (accessed March 3, 2009).

p. 68, "The suspects had hoped . . .": Isabel Kershner, "New U.S.-Israeli Crime Ring Detailed," *New York Times*, August 3, 2009, www.nytimes.com/2009/08/04/world/middleeast/04israel.html (accessed August 8, 2009).

p. 69, "The Identity Theft Resource Center . . .": Identity Theft Resource Center, "Fact Sheet 301: Enhancing Law Enforcement," August 21, 2009 www.idtheftcenter.org/artman2/publish/law_communicate/Fact_Sheet_301Enhancing_Law_Enforcement.shtml (accessed August 10, 2009).

p. 69, "Thieves often use false identities . . .": Judith M. Collins, *Investigating Identity Theft: A Guide for Businesses, Law Enforcement, and Victims*, Hoboken, NJ: John Wiley & Sons, 2006, 71.

p. 69, "One study of law enforcement . . .": U.S. Department of Justice, "Law Enforcement Issues and Response," Office of Justice Programs, July 2007, www.ojp.usdoj.gov/nij/publications/id-theft/law-issues.htm (accessed August 10, 2009).

p. 70, "The Consumer Sentinel ID Theft . . .": Colorado Attorney General Office, "What Can Law Enforcement Do to Help Victims of Identity Theft?" 2008, www.ago.state.co.us/idtheft/lehelp.cfm.html (accessed August 10, 2009).

p. 70, "In July 2008 . . .": U.S. Department of Justice, "U.S. Attorney Pat Meehan Announces Identity Theft Enforcement System,"

July 10, 2008, www.usdoj.gov/usao/pae/News/Pr/2008/jul/niclerelease.pdf (accessed December 8, 2008).

pp. 70–71, "However, the number of official . . .": Wisconsin Department of Agriculture, Trade, and Consumer Protection, "The State of Privacy in the State," www.datcp.state.wi.us/privacy/index.jsp (accessed August 8. 2009).

p. 72, "Anything less than that . . .": Daniel Solove, Marc Rotenberg, and Paul M. Schwartz, *Privacy, Information, and Technology*, New York: Aspen Publishers, 2006, 253.

Chapter 5

p. 75, "In 2003 office retailers . . .": Laura Knowles and Tim Mekeel, "A Shred of Protections; Sales of Shredders Have Increased Dramatically, Retailers Say, as the Public Becomes More Aware of The Danger of Identity Theft from Discarded Personal Documents and Credit Cards," *Lancaster New Era*, March 29, 2004.

p. 77, "It is important to keep . . .": Daniel J. Solove, Marc Rotenberg, and Paul M. Schwartz, *Privacy, Information, and Technology*, New York: Aspen Publishers, 2006, 263.

p. 78, "But in reality, those expenses . . .": Andrew Johnson, "Lifelock Tries to Fend Off Legal Battles," *The Arizona Republic*, August 17, 2009, www.azcentral.com/arizonarepublic/news/articles/2009/08/17/20090817biz-lifelock0817.html (accessed August 25, 2009).

p. 79, "The three credit reporting . . .": Christine Dugas, "More Banks Offer Free Help to Victims of Identity Theft," *USA Today*, January 19, 2007, www.usatoday.com/money/industries/banking/2007-01-19-bank-id-theft_x.htm (accessed February 20, 2009).

p. 79, "In addition, it is smart . . .": Federal Trade Commission, "Detect Identity Theft," www.ftc.gov/bcp/edu/microsites/idtheft/consumers/detect.html#ShouldIuseacreditmonitoringservice (accessed March 13, 2009).

p. 80, "But the government cautions . . .": Federal Trade Commission, "Free Annual Credit Reports," March 9, 2009, www.ftc.gov/freereports (accessed May 13, 2009).

p. 80, "These costs can include . . .": Herb Weisbaum, "Why ID Theft Insurance Might Not Be Worth It," MSNBC.COM, May 8, 2006, www.msnbc.msn.com/id/12692565/ns/business-consumer_news (accessed March 13, 2009).

p. 80, "For most people . . .": Weisbaum, "Why ID Theft Insurance Might Not Be Worth It," May 8, 2006.

p. 82, "A large number of people . . .": Identity Theft Resource Center, "Workplace Facts and Statistics," 2009, www.idtheftcenter.org/workplace_facts.html (accessed March 26, 2009).

p. 82, "Another study reported . . .": Identity Theft Resource Center, "Workplace Facts and Statistics," 2009.

p. 82, "The program is a service . . .": "New Certification Seal Identifies Merchants Committed to Fighting Identity Theft," *PR Newswire*, March 2, 2009.

p. 82, "Generally these services do not . . .": "Identity Theft Resolution Services Provided by Identity Theft 911 to First National Bank at Paris Customers," *Business Wire*, May 20, 2009.

p. 82, "A secure payment agent . . .": Identity Theft Resource Center, "ITRC 2009 Consumer Awareness Survey: The Need for 'Secure Payment Agent' (SPA)," May 19, 2009, www.idtheftcenter.org/artman2/publish/lib_survey/SPA_White_Paper.shtml (accessed May 26, 2009).

p. 83, "For additional fees . . .": "Identity Theft Protection," Discover Card, 2009, www.discovercard.com/protection-solutions/identity theft.html (accessed March 13, 2009).

p. 84, "In addition, this law requires . . .": Federal Reserve Board, "Electronic Fund Transfers," August 16, 2007, www.federalreserve.gov/pubs/consumerhdbk/electronic.htm#loss (accessed March 13, 2009).

p. 84, "Second, if consumers dispute . . .": U.S. Department of Justice, "U.S. Attorney Pat Meehan Announces Identity Theft Enforcement System," July 10, 2008, www.usdoj.gov/usao/pae/News/Pr/2008/jul/niclerelease.pdf (accessed December 8, 2008).

p. 85, "Hawaii is one state . . .": Federal Trade Commission, "The Fair Credit Reporting Act," June 2008, www.ftc.gov/os/statutes/fcradoc.pdf (accessed March 13, 2009).

p. 85, "And FCRA is broad enough . . .": Jonathan D. Glater, "Another Hurdle for the Jobless: Credit Inquiries," August 6, 2009, www.nytimes.com/2009/08/07/business/07credit.html?_r=2&hp (accessed August 10, 2009).

p. 86, "Those policies may include . . .": Steve Weisman, *50 Ways to Protect Your Identity and Your Credit*, Upper Saddle River, NJ: Prentice Hall, 2005, 83.

p. 86, "Generally, under this law . . .": Federal Trade Commission, "Prepared Statement of the Federal Trade Commission on Identity Theft Before the Committee on Banking and Financial Services, United States House of Representatives," September 13, 2000, www.ftc.gov/os/2000/09/idthefttest.htm (accessed March 11, 2009).

p. 87, "Only .5 percent . . .": Solove, Rotenberg, and Schwartz, *Privacy, Information, and Technology*, 2006, 267.

p. 87, "Please be advised that . . .": Weisman, *50 Ways to Protect Your Identity and Your Credit*, 198.

p. 88, "One, verify the identity . . .": U.S. Treasury Department, "Treasury and Federal Financial Regulators Issue Final Patriot Act Regulations on Customer Identification," April 30, 2003, www.ustreas.gov/press/releases/js335.htm (accessed March 15, 2009).

p. 88, "Regarding financial records . . .": Solove, Rotenberg, and Schwartz, *Privacy, Information, and Technology*, 2006, 279.

p. 88, "These letters are called . . .": Solove, Rotenberg, and Schwartz, *Privacy, Information, and Technology*, 2006, 280.

p. 89, "Legislators fear that if this were allowed to happen . . .": Solove, Rotenberg, and Schwartz, *Privacy, Information, and Technology*, 2006, 263.

p. 89, "FACTA states that . . .": Judith M. Collins, *Investigating Identity Theft: A Guide for Businesses, Law Enforcement, and Victims*, Hoboken, NJ: John Wiley & Sons, 2006, 76.

p. 89, "Under the law . .": Michael J. Arata Jr., *Preventing Identity Theft for Dummies*, Indianapolis: Wiley Publishing, Inc., 2004, 46–47.

p. 90, "These types of businesses . . .": Federal Trade Commission, "Fighting Fraud with the Red Flags Rule: A How-To Guide for Business," March 2009. www.ftc.gov/bcp/edu/pubs/business/idtheft/bus23.pdf (accessed May 10, 2009).

p. 91, "The number of data breaches . . .": Identity Theft Resource Center, "Security Breaches 2008," March 26, 2009, www.idtheft center.org/artman2/publish/lib_survey/Breaches_2008.shtml (accessed May 21, 2009).

p. 91, "As of June 2009 . . .": "Notice of Security State Breach Laws," financialprivacynow.org, January 7, 2009, www.consumersunion.org/campaigns//financialprivacynow/002215indiv.html (accessed April 21, 2009).

p. 92, "Some states require . . .": "Consumers Union's Guide to Security Freeze Protection," Financialprivacynow.org, April 6, 2009, www.consumersunion.org/campaigns/learn_more/003484indiv.html (accessed April 21, 2009).

p. 92, "Smaller businesses may have to . . .": Ben Worthen, "New Data Privacy Laws Set for Firms," *Wall Street Journal*, October 16, 2008.

Chapter 6

p. 94, "When it comes to preferred . . .": "Unisys Research Shows U.S. Consumers Overwhelmingly Trust Biometrics for Data Protection," *Business Wire*, December 9, 2008.

p. 96, "However, the company offering . . .": "Shoppers, You Can't Touch This," *Chicago Tribune*, March 21, 2008.

p. 96, "A person being scanned . . .": Steve Weisman, *50 Ways to Protect Your Identity and Your Credit*, Upper Saddle River, NJ: Prentice Hall, 2005, 71.

p. 98, "However, if a pupil is dilated . . .": Weisman, *50 Ways to Protect Your Identity and Your Credit*, 70.

p. 98, "Cairo Amman Bank . . .": "Banking on Biometrics in the Twinkle of an Eye. IrisGuard Is Transforming the Way We Conduct Our Banking Transactions," *Business Wire*, April 14, 2008.

p. 98, "In some cases, these players . . .": Alan Schwarz, "A Future in Baseball, Hinging on DNA," *New York Times*, July 22, 2009, www.nytimes.com/2009/07/23/sports/baseball/23dna.html?_r=1&partner=rss&emc=rss (accessed August 15, 2009).

p. 99, "However, it is not clear . . .": Michael S. Schmidt and Alan Schwarz, "Baseball's Use of DNA Raises Questions," *New York Times*, July 21, 2009, www.nytimes.com/2009/07/22/sports/baseball/22dna.html?ref=baseball (accessed August 15, 2009).

p. 101, "Some of the more recent . . .": Cassie Shaner, "Morgantown's 'Modern Marvel': History Channel Program Visits Biometric Office," *McClatchy - Tribune Business News*, May 17, 2009.

p. 101, "Other devices measure . . .": Weisman, *50 Ways to Protect Your Identity and Your Credit*, 69.

p. 101, "The Pew Research Center . . .": Pew Research Center, "Americans Taking Abramoff, Alito and Domestic Spying in Stride," January 11, 2006, http://people-press.org/report/267/americans-taking-abramoff-alito-and-domestic-spying-in-stride (accessed August 15, 2009).

p. 102, "Advocates said the trade-off . . .": John R. Vacca, *Identity Theft*, Upper Saddle River, NJ: Prentice Hall, 2003, 342.

Chapter 7

p. 103, "Countries that are often host . . .": John R. Vacca, *Identity Theft*, Upper Saddle River, NJ: Prentice Hall, 2003, 399.

p. 103, "A recent report showed . . .": "Identity Theft Twice as Likely in Canada, the U.K., and the U.S. than in Other European Countries," *Canada NewsWire*, October 21, 2008.

p. 103, "Though hard data is not . . .": Liz Pulliam Weston, "What Europe Can Teach Us About Identity Theft," MSNBC.COM, http://moneycentral.msn.com/content/Banking/FinancialPrivacy/P116528.asp (accessed March 11, 2009).

p. 104, "The process to authorize credit . . .": Weston, "What Europe Can Teach Us."

p. 105, "European laws are stricter . . .": Weston, "What Europe Can Teach Us."

p. 105, "Canada does not have any nationwide . . .": "Identity Fraud Has Struck 1.7 Million Canadians," *The Gazette,* Montreal, Quebec, November 18, 2008.

p. 105, "Canada does not have any antispam . . .": Michael Geist, "Lawless Canada a Haven for Spammers," *The Ottawa Citizen*, December 2, 2008.

p. 105, "By early 2008 . . .": Mark Townsend, "Four Million Britons Have Fallen Victim to Identity Fraud. Are You Next?," *The Observer*, December 9, 2007.

p. 106, "If the crime does not involve . . .": United Kingdom Home Office, "Identity Fraud and Theft," August 6, 2008, www.crimereduction.homeoffice.gov.uk/fraud/fraud17.htm (accessed March 15, 2009).

p. 106, "Sweden and Finland . . .": Vacca, *Identity Theft*, 2003, 402.

p. 107, "If people wanted . . .": Vacca, *Identity Theft*, 2003, 402.

p. 107, "For example, in 2005 . . .": David Pallister, "Three Guilty of Identity Fraud Which Netted Millions," *The Guardian*, December 1, 2006.

p. 107, "The organization looks at . . .": IdentityTheft.org.uk, "Identity Theft: Don't Become a Victim," 2009, www.identitytheft. org.uk/what-is-being-done.asp (accessed March 18, 2009).

p. 107, "Because of the new measures . . .": National Fraud Strategic Authority, "The National Fraud Strategy: A New Approach to Combating Fraud, 2009-2011," United Kingdom Attorney General's Office, www.insurancefraudbureau.org/files/misc_pdfs/ nfsa_strategy_aw_11.03@2.pdf (accessed March 11, 2009).

p. 107, "These criminals were charged . . .": National Fraud Strategic Authority, "The National Fraud Strategy," 46.

p. 107, "That year, police uncovered . . .": Phyllis Tsang, "Credit Agency Offers Warning on Identity Theft," *South China Morning Post*, May 4, 2009.

p. 108, "Hong Kong officials also urge . . .": Tsang, "Credit Agency Offers Warning," May 4, 2009.

p. 108, "While similar cases in the past . . .": Cheng Zhiliang and Li Baojie, "Police officer's daughter enters university in name of classmate, evoking nationwide outcry," *China View*, October 5, 2009, http://bbs.chinadaily.com.cn/viewthread.php?tid=637561 (accessed January 13, 2010).

p. 110, "In the Philippines . . .": "Philippine Official Warns Banks Over Rise of Technology-Related Crimes," BBC Monitoring Asia Pacific, April 20, 2009.

p. 110, "The government has also created . . .": Australian Government, Attorney General's Office, "Identity Security," June 12, 2008, www.ag.gov.au/www/agd/agd.nsf/Page/Crimeprevention_ Identitysecurity (accessed March 18, 2009).

p. 111, "The Identity Theft Resource Center . . .": Identity Theft Resource Center, "Fact Sheet 122: Identity Theft Travel Tips," May 1, 2007, www.idtheftmostwanted.org/artman2/publish/c_ tips/Fact_Sheet_122_Identity_Theft_Travel_Tips.shtml (accessed March 26, 2009).

p. 112, "Those operating through . . .": Brian Krebs, "Mapping the Russian Business Network." *Washington Post*, October 13, 2007, http://voices.washingtonpost.com/securityfix/2007/10/mapping_the_russian_business_n.html (accessed February, 2009).

p. 112, "In 2006 users of the network . . .": Brian Krebs, "Shadowy Russian Firm Seen as Conduit for Cybercrime," *Washington Post*, October 13, 2007, www.washingtonpost.com/wp-dyn/content/article/2007/10/12/AR2007101202461.html (accessed February 26, 2009).

p. 112, "But RBN's antispyware . . .": Rhys Blakely, Jonathan Richards, and Tony Halpin, "Cybergang Raises Fear of New Crime Wave, *The Times*, London, November 10, 2007, http://technology.timesonline.co.uk/tol/news/tech_and_web/the_web/articles2844031.ece (accessed February 26, 2009).

p. 112, "Experts believe the group . . .": Krebs, "Shadowy Russian Firm Seen as Conduit for Cybercrime," October 13, 2007.

p. 113, "The ringleader is thought to be . . .": Joseph Menn and Andrea Chang, "11 Charged in Massive Identity Theft," *Los Angeles Times*, August 6, 2008.

Further Information

Books

Arata, Michael J. Jr. *Preventing Identity Theft for Dummies.* Indianapolis, IN: Wiley Publishing, Inc., 2004.

Weisman, Steve. *50 Ways to Protect Your Identity and Your Credit.* Upper Saddle River, NJ: Prentice Hall, 2005.

Wilson, Michael R. *Frequently Asked Questions about Identity Theft.* New York: Rosen Publishing Group, 2007.

Credit Bureaus

Equifax: 1-800-685-1111; www.equifax.com; P.O. Box 740241, Atlanta, GA 30374-0241.

Experian: 1-888-397-3742; www.experian.com; P.O. Box 9532, Allen, TX 75013.

TransUnion: 1-800-916-8800; www.transunion.com; P.O. Box 6790, Fullerton, CA 92834-6790.

Government Agencies

Federal Trade Commission

Responsible for protecting U.S. consumers when it comes to financial and monetary issues.

www.ftc.gov/idtheft/

State Attorneys General Offices

In each state, an attorney general oversees state laws as they relate to consumers. An attorney general's website will often give consumers information about the latest scams (identity scams and others) and provide a number or web address for lodging complaints.

www.naag.org/

United States Department of Justice

Responsible for fighting identity theft that occurs on a federal level.

www.usdoj.gov/criminal/fraud/websites/idtheft.html

Junk Mail Opt-out Agencies

Direct Marketing Association
Mail Preference Service
P.O. Box 282
Carmel, NY 10512

Dunn & Bradstreet
Customer Service
899 Eaton Ave.
Bethlehem, PA 18025

Metromail Corporation
List Maintenance
901 West Bond
Lincoln, NE 68521

R.L. Polk & Co.–Name Deletion File
List Compilation Development
26955 Northwestern Hwy
Southfield, MI 48034-4716

Database America
Compilation Department
470 Chestnut Ridge Road
Woodcliff, NJ 07677

Websites

Anti-Phishing Working Group
The Anti-Phishing Working Group is a network of businesses and companies who are committed to fighting phishing scams.
www.antiphishing.org

Identity Theft Resource Center
The Identity Theft Resource Center, based in San Diego, California, holds a variety of information including the latest scam alerts, state and local resources, and statistics. The organization provides a toll-free number that victims can call if they've been targeted by identity thieves. The number is (888) 400-5530. Victims can also email victims@idtheftcenter.org
www.idtheftcenter.org

Federal Trade Commission
Victims can report identity theft by calling 1-877-ID-THEFT (438-4338), or fill out an online form.
www.ftc.gov.

National Crime Prevention Council.
"Preventing Identity Theft: A Guide for Consumers."
www.ncpc.org/resources/files/pdf/fraud/idtheftrev.pdf

Privacy Rights Clearinghouse
The Privacy Rights Clearinghouse was founded in 1992 and is dedicated to giving consumers information about their privacy rights.
www.privacyrights.org

Bibliography

Abagnale, Frank W. *Catch Me If You Can: The True Story of a Real Fake.* New York: Broadway, 2000.

Arata, Michael J. Jr. *Preventing Identity Theft for Dummies.* Indianapolis: Wiley Publishing, Inc., 2004.

Collins, Judith M. *Investigating Identity Theft: A Guide for Businesses, Law Enforcement, and Victims.* Hoboken, NJ. John Wiley & Sons, 2006.

Federal Trade Commission. *Consumer Sentinel Network Data Book for January-December 2008.* Washington, D.C.: Federal Trade Commission, February 2009.

Federal Trade Commission. "Fighting Back Against Identity Theft." www.ftc.gov/bcp/edu/microsites/idtheft/ (accessed January 14, 2010).

Identity Theft Resource Center. "Working to Resolve Identity Theft." www.idtheftcenter.org (accessed January 14, 2010).

Solove, Daniel J., Marc Rotenberg, and Paul M. Schwartz. *Privacy, Information, and Technology.* New York: Aspen Publishers, 2006.

Stewart, Gail. *Crime Scene Investigations: Identity Theft.* San Diego, CA: Lucent Books, 2007.

Synovate. "Federal Trade Commission 2006 Identity Theft Survey Report." McLean, VA: Synovate, November 2007.

United States Department of Justice. "Identity Theft and Identity Fraud." www.usdoj.gov/criminal/fraud/websites/idtheft.html (accessed January 14, 2010).

Vacca, John R. *Identity Theft.* Upper Saddle River, NJ: Prentice Hall, 2003.

Weisman, Steve. *50 Ways to Protect Your Identity and Your Credit.* Upper Saddle River, NJ: Prentice Hall, 2005.

Wilson, Michael R. *Frequently Asked Questions about Identity Theft.* New York: Rosen Publishing Group, 2007.

Index

Page numbers in **boldface** are illustrations, tables, and charts.

About the Author

RACHAEL HANEL has written more than twenty nonfiction books for children and teaches journalism, English, and history at the college level. She is working on a memoir about growing up as a gravedigger's daughter in southern Minnesota. She lives and works in Madison Lake, Minnesota. This is her first book for Marshall Cavendish Benchmark.